SPIRITUAL WARRIOR II
Transforming Lust Into Love

B.T. SWAMI

HARI NAMA PRESS

Copyright © 1998 by John E. Favors

All rights reserved. No part of this book may be reproduced, stored in a retrieval system, or transmitted in any form, by any means, including mechanical, electronic, photocopying, recording, or otherwise, without prior written consent of the publisher.

Hari-Nama Press gratefully acknowledges the BBT for the use of verses and purports from Srila Prabhupada's books. All such verses and purports are © Bhaktivedanta Book Trust International, Inc.

The publisher gratefully acknowledges the kind permission of Goloka Books in allowing us the use of their artwork for incorporation into our cover design.

First printing 1998
Second edition printing 2005
Third edition printing: Amazon KDP 2020

Cover and interior design by Subala dasa / Ecstatic Creations
Cover artwork by Philip Malpass / Goloka Books

ISBN 9798639618390

SPIRITUAL WARRIOR II

Transforming Lust Into Love

Dedication

I dedicate this book to three people who taught me the magic of transforming lust into love: my mother, Mother Pearline; my uncle, Nanda Maharaja; and my spiritual father, Srila Prabhupada.

I can never thank each of you enough for your unconditional love.

Contents

Acknowledgments 1
Foreword 3
Editor's Preface............................... 7
Author's Preface 9
Introduction: The School of Love 13
   Love Satisfies the Starvation • Our Natural
   Position • The Dynamics of the School of Love •
   Genuine Teachers Can Enthuse Their Students •
   The Correlation between Love and Happiness •
   Useless Substitutes for Love • We Cannot Cheat •
   Dependence on the Lord

Chapter 1: Sex and the Leadership Crisis 27
   Lust, Sex, and Leadership • Misused Sexuality
   Is the Cause • Society Encourages Sense
   Gratification • Consequences of Misdirected Sexual
   Energy • Bisexuality and Homosexuality • Spiritual

Aspects of Homosexuality • Other Esoteric Aspects of Sexuality • How to Remedy the Situation • Subtle Sex • Sexual Energy and Peace • The Power of Sexual Energy • An Unfortunate Example • Abuses of Power • The Proper Role of Leaders • The Importance of Boundaries • This Is War • Questions and Answers

Chapter 2: What Is Love? 51
The World Lacks Love • Love Is Not About Getting Something • Love Is Not a Feeling • Love Is Not Always Pleasant • Jealousy and Envy Are Not Love • Love Is Stronger than Doubt • The Source of Love • Unconditional Love Is Spiritual • A Gathering of Sages • Love Is Unmotivated Service • Becoming Transcendental • Daily Life Is a Training Ground • Questions and Answers

Chapter 3: What Is Lust?....................... 73
Suffering in the Material World • The Material Universe Is Not Our Home • We Are Accountable • The Gradual Path of Degradation • Other Ways Lust Tricks Us • Triumphing Over Lust • Spiritual Strength Conquers the Senses • The Supersoul in the Heart • Passing the Lord's Tests • The Temptation of Jesus • Different Degrees of Lust • Importance of the Human Form • God's Help Is Always Available • Questions and Answers

Chapter 4: The Power of Sense Gratification 99
Developing the Higher Taste • A Parable: The Mouse and the Sage • The Power of False Ego • Detachment • Friends Help Us Evolve • The Dark Night of the Soul • Turning Negatives into Positives • The Importance of Faith • A Hospital for Our Spiritual Diseases • Become the Lord's

Slave and Be Free • Material Concerns Can Be
Distractions • Our Interaction with Higher Beings •
Intense Spiritual Pleasure • Three Requirements for
Spiritual Peace • Questions and Answers

Chapter 5: Sexuality in Everyday Life 125
Importance of Deep Relationships • Beauty
Comes from the Soul • Sex Is Sacred • The Power
of Sexual Energy • Sexuality in Marriage • The
Science of Procreation • Natural Sexuality • How
a Soul Chooses its Circumstances • Karma and
Free Will • The Practice of Celibacy • Celibacy Is
Not Denial • Renunciation Takes Various Forms •
Celibacy in Marriage • Placing Material Life in
Perspective • Questions and Answers

Chapter 6: Love Between a Man and a Woman 145
Lack of Depth in Today's Society • Loving
Others Means Loving Ourselves • The Quest for
Wholeness • Distorted Gender Roles • Spiritual Life
Is Androgynous • Resolving Differences • Offering
Everything Back to the Lord • Are We Really
Selfless? • Attachment and Detachment • Looking
for a Mate • Seventeen Practices for Attaining
Success in the School of Love • Questions and
Answers

Chapter 7: Loving Our Neighbors 173
The Need for a Culture of Love • Loving Our
Neighbors Goes beyond the Surface • Loving
and Trusting Others • Keeping Secrets •
Confidentiality • The Value of Making Judgments •
Absolute Criteria of Spiritual Life • Laws Are
Universal • Evaluate Ourselves First • How to
Remain Positive • Negative Behavior Is a Call for
Love • Dealing with Negativity in Others • Dealing

with Racism, Nationalism, and Genderism • Developing Meaningful Service • The Goal Is to Become Transcendental • The Struggle with Illusion • Questions and Answers

Chapter 8: The Practice of Compassion **201**
A Prerequisite for Returning Home • Beyond the Salvationist Mentality • The Meaning of Compassion • Compassion Is Not Condescending • Compassion Requires Courage • Those with Physical Challenges • The Homeless • Those in Confinement • The Plight of Refugees • The Abused • How Compassionate Are We? • Compassion Is Spiritually Empowering • Help for the Disillusioned • Insufficient Love Is the Problem • Becoming Receptive to Higher Energies • The Art of Self-renewal • Questions and Answers

Chapter 9: Love of God **227**
Longing for the Lord • Love of God Is Not a Demand • Fear of God • Doubts about God • Levels of God-realization • We Need Deep Spiritual Experiences • Look For the Inner Teachings • Love of God Is Intoxicating • Personal Association with God in the World's Traditions • Spiritual Union • Confidential Aspects of Spirituality • The Realm of Eternal Romance • Go Deep Into Your Own Tradition • Spiritual Life Is Our Rightful Claim • Questions and Answers

Closing Reflections **253**
Glossary **257**
Endnotes **261**
Index **263**
About the Author **267**

Acknowledgments

I would like to express my deep appreciation to all the people who dedicated time and effort to make this book possible. Greg Gurewitz reproduced countless tapes so that others might transcribe them. Bonnie Brown, Glenn Burns, Leslie Dent-Gurewitz, Amanda Dowling, Paul Ewing, Willetta Ewing, Danny Gurewitz, Patricia Jackson, Dawn Lamky, Tina Pihaylic, Laurice Stewart, and Brenda Williams carefully transcribed the tapes from which the text was taken. Paulette Bowles, Makeda Cannon, Lisa DeSoto, Adam Kenney, Robyn Terry, William Webb, Marilyn Wood, Lauren Kossis, and Krista Oliver provided invaluable editing assistance. Stewart Cannon did the wonderful layout and cover design. I would also like to thank Ajamila dasa of Goloka Books for his generosity in allowing us to use a drawing from the first volume of *Illustrated Bhagavatam Stories* as part of the cover design. I would like to thank Reshma Mahendra, Edward Anobah, and Chetna Kang for financing the printing of this book.

Without all of your hard work and love, this book could not have come into being. I love you all, because you are most lovable.

Foreword

Spiritual Warrior II: Transforming Lust into Love is a book to savor and treasure, a book that needs to be read and reread because of its spiritual potency and priceless value for everyday living. I receive so many books in the mail to read and, I am sorry to say, the vast majority of them have little or no substance, simply being combinations of words strung together to entertain the mind and, perhaps, the intelligence. You can imagine how happy and excited I was as I began to read *Spiritual Warrior II* and found myself saying, "Yes, yes! This is what I need. This is what I choose to learn and apply."

It is with great pleasure that I offer my reactions to Bhakti Tirtha Swami's unique, easy-to-understand presentation of the ancient, eternal teachings included in this book. Although I have never met B.T. Swami personally—an occasion I look forward to—in a sense I have already met him through his previous books and an audiotape of one of his lectures. His courage to speak the deepest truths and his wealth of knowledge has impressed me greatly. As a writer, minister, and speaker myself, I am familiar with the tendency to say what pleases people so that they will continue to listen and attend classes. B.T. Swami cuts right to the core of our problems and offers real, eternal solutions that transcend the mundane beliefs and rhetoric of the average religious leader or politician.

The book's combination of primarily, but not exclusively, Christian, Muslim, and Vedic teachings is for serious students who genuinely desire to know who they are, how to live in harmony with God's laws, and how to love God and achieve success as a human being. The lessons the author shares so generously are the difficult ones, not how to catch a man, how to keep a woman, or even how to use God and His universe to get what you want. All these benefits come naturally when you love—not when you use, but when you love.

Those of any religion who care about themselves and truly desire to fulfill their mission as human beings will devour the knowledge that jumps off every page of *Spiritual Warrior II*. Some books give us an "ah-ha!" or two, or one interesting point to apply, which may be enough to justify the price of the book and the time spent reading it. Here, it happens every paragraph, and sometimes every line! I am currently on my second and even third reading of certain chapters of this divinely inspired offering.

Everyone needs a copy of this book. Couples and families need to read it together, comment on its lessons, and discuss ways in which they can apply these powerful truths to their communications and interactions. Schools need to include this book in their psychology classes, for it goes beyond the mundane psychology of analyzing illness and aims directly at the heart and core of every issue, which is love of God. Without

God, no system will ever bring a utopia, because we cannot live a heavenly life by keeping the owner and proprietor, God, on the outside while we are on the inside living off of His kingdom. With God in the center, all is possible, and life is blissful, loving, and prosperous.

At some point in our lives, each of us must wake up and face the challenge of being who we truly are, and of bringing forth and expressing this true self from moment to moment. The only way we can solve the problems of life, which we ultimately can do, is to have eternal knowledge and truth and to apply this knowledge under any and all circumstances.

Whatever we have in life is what we have earned. If you desire love, bliss, and liberation, I suggest you start here with this book.

God bless you, B.T. Swami, and thank you, my friend, for your enormous gift to us all.

> —Terry Cole-Whittaker, D.D., author of: *What You Think of Me Is None of My Business*; *How to Have More in a Have-not World*; *The Inner Path from Where You Are to Where You Want to Be*; and *Love and Power in a World Without Limits*

Editor's Preface

Spiritual Warrior II: Transforming Lust into Love consists of lectures given by Bhakti Tirtha Swami to a wide variety of audiences over a period of several years. Because the topics were originally presented in spoken form, the style is conversational and informal. In the editing process, we have modified the text to enhance readability, yet sought to preserve some of the verbal nuances that would maintain the mood of the original presentation. By so doing, we hope to create an atmosphere that literally makes you part of the audience, where you can experience the powerful presence of the speaker, B.T. Swami, as he shares essential nourishment for the soul.

We would like to mention a few other stylistic considerations. As B.T. Swami examines the issues of lust and love, he includes various perspectives from many different spiritual philosophies. At times he uses Sanskrit terminology from the Vedas, a vast body of ancient scriptures originating from the area of the world known today as India. The text explains the meaning of these Sanskrit terms, and for convenience a glossary at the end of this book also defines them. Finally, the end of each chapter includes a few of the many questions and answers exchanged during the original lectures. We hope that these will respond to some of the concerns that may arise for you in the course of reading this material. These discussions between B.T. Swami and the audience may also give you different angles from which to view the topics presented.

This book is the second edition of the second volume in our *Spiritual Warrior* series of lectures by B.T. Swami. *Spiritual Warrior I: Uncovering Spiritual Truths in Psychic Phenomena*, *Spiritual Warrior III: Solace for the Heart in Difficult Times*, *Spiritual Warrior IV: Conquering the Enemies of the Mind*, *Spiritual Warrior V: Making the Mind Your Best Friend*, and *Spiritual Warrior VI: Beyond Fanaticism, Terrorism, and War: Discover the Peace Solution* are already in print, and several more volumes are planned. The information presented within these pages is extremely rare, and we hope you will make the most of the knowledge they contain. If you take these teachings seriously, they can transform your life into a most sublime, loving adventure.

Author's Preface

Famine, disease, terrorism, war, murder, suicide, storms, floods, earthquakes, volcanic eruptions, toxic rivers, poisoned food, dying trees—this planet is presenting us with numerous symptoms of serious imbalance. Yet despite the widespread physical suffering throughout the world today, ultimately the difficulties confronting us are not material, but spiritual. These problems reflect our failure to fulfill our deepest longings to love and be loved, and any solution will require more than just a sophisticated technological effort. We may have made great scientific progress, but as a culture we still have little understanding of love and even less appreciation for the spiritual dimensions of life. The strife and destruction that surround us point to an urgent need to remedy this situation. We must learn how to love ourselves, and also how to love our home planet and the other living beings who reside here with us.

The resolute material orientation of industrial culture has

led us down a blind alley. Consumer society has encouraged us to indulge our desires to the utmost and to seek the fulfillment of our desires at every opportunity. Instead of developing self-knowledge and self-mastery, we have learned to look outside ourselves in a never-ending quest for gratification, mistakenly believing that such a pursuit can ensure our happiness. Yet we are discovering that those who "have everything" can still be profoundly miserable and lead desperate, empty lives. Something has gone seriously wrong.

The problem is that we have dedicated ourselves to satisfying our lust rather than expressing our love. Although we are all inherently loving beings, we have forgotten our true nature and sacrificed our birthright for a seductive substitute that ultimately brings us pain rather than joy. Because our collective goal has become to gratify our physical senses above all else, we have developed a self-centered culture that condones competition, exploitation, and "whatever it takes" to get us what we want. Our egocentric behavior manifests in countless forms and is driven by lust. For example, we may engage in sexual activity without love, dominate others in order to feel powerful, destroy rainforests to create more profitable grazing land, manipulate financial markets for personal gain, lie and cheat to gain political prominence, take drugs to get high, or ignore our own children in favor of making more money.

Spiritual Warrior II: Transforming Lust into Love is an attempt to examine the topics of lust and love in depth. The book's premise is that we must gain a spiritual understanding of lust and love if we are to live healthier, more productive, and more fulfilled lives. In what follows, we will explore the meaning, manifestations, and dangers of lust; suggest ways to overcome its power; and describe in detail the progressive levels of love that culminate in love of and service to God.

The Introduction describes life as a school of love—an environment ultimately designed to prepare us to once again become deep unconditional lovers. We emphasize how everyone here is starving for love even though we are made for love. The first chapter describes the world's crisis in leadership—a situation that has a profound impact on all of us. The examples of our leaders filter down into the rest of society and set the tone for how we live. Now more than ever, we have a desperate need for leaders who have learned to conquer their lust and fulfill their responsibilities with love. All of us are leaders in one capacity or another, and we can all benefit from conquering our lust and becoming more loving in every aspect of our lives. The rest of the book shows how to accomplish this. Chapters 2 and 3 define lust and love in more detail and provide a basic understanding of how they operate. Chapter 4 looks at sense gratification and its various ramifications, while Chapter 5 specifically discusses the role of sexuality in our lives. Chapter 6 is dedicated to examining loving relationships between men and women, and Chapter 7 explains how to develop love in all our other relationships. Chapters 8 and 9 explore two more deeply spiritual aspects of love: compassion and love of God.

These challenging times require us to fortify ourselves with spiritual knowledge and, even more important, we must put our knowledge into practice. Only then can we call ourselves spiritual warriors capable of serving others. As spiritual warriors, we must never forget that our greatest ally is love and our most dangerous enemy is lust. We can be of genuine service only if we are free from selfish desires and available to become pure vehicles for God's love.

May this book help you master the seductive illusions of lust and become a spiritual warrior radiating divine love to all you encounter.

Introduction

The School of Love

Love Satisfies the Starvation

Life is a school of love. In this school, we are not just hungry, but starving for love. Starvation is a life-threatening affair. A person in this predicament wants to survive, but if they do not get food and water, in time they will fall sick and even die. Just think of the difficulty involved in trying to live a so-called normal life if you don't have food, water, or proper shelter. It is very difficult. If we take this reflection a step further, we realize that our real nourishment and shelter is love, because the soul is made for love.

Ultimately, life is about spiritual expressions, which involve completeness, knowledge, and happiness. These spiritual expressions will manifest as we recognize our eternal nature. We are eternal beings, which means that we are not meant to have temporary experiences. If we think of ourselves as temporary entities, it will consequently mean that our goals will also be temporary. However, since we are eternal beings, our activities are ultimately meant to be eternal.

As we endeavor to satisfy the different demands of the body, we are looking for certain experiences, facilities, and relationships that can counteract our deeper starvation and satisfy the hunger. We ultimately want relationships because we want a community of love. We want to live a full life because life itself is really a love affair. It means that when we are not in loving environments or relationships, we are having real problems with the quality of our existence. As a matter of fact, when we think of different emotions, we will see even more distinctly how life is a school of love and how it is ultimately expressed in its fullness through the goals of religion, which aim at satisfying the Lord. That which satisfies the Lord actually satisfies the soul.

Our Natural Position

We do a lot of pretending and playing God instead of recognizing that we are made for love and that we are loved deeper than we could ever imagine by the Supreme. If we really accept that we are most loveable, how could we ever get depressed? If we really accept that we are made for love and loved deeply, could we be inactive? We would never feel any moroseness because there would always be opportunities for us to receive love and to give love. If we really accept that life is a school of love, how could we not be mindful at every moment? We would constantly try to get nourishment that helps us act according to our natural position. Just as a machine functions best when used properly according to its purpose, we also give the best results when we function according to our purpose. Conversely, when a machine has a specific purpose and we use it in an inappropriate way, we will create many problems.

When we are not happy, it means that we are forgetting our identity and purpose. Our dissatisfaction means that we are missing opportunities to share love, to give love, and to receive love. For instance, whenever we fall into a depression, it is a sign that we are not sending out enough love. This is the school of love. Some people fail again and again because they somehow do not understand. Some people have very exciting points in their lives and, at other times, extremely complex periods. It means that sometimes they are getting it and sometimes they are not. Some people try to find that love only within one person. They try to find that love only within one activity, race, religion, or political group. They just do not get it because, being made for love, they cannot get nourishment in only one particular way at only a specific time. They must have it always and it must come from so many sectors. Not only must it come from many directions, but they must also give it in so many ways. On the other hand, some people are excited by a life of love. They see each moment as an opportunity to experience more of what they are already experiencing. Somehow they get it.

The Dynamics of the School of Love

Think about the dynamics of a school. A school is a place comprised of students and teachers. We are all students, and sometimes as a part of our own learning, we are teaching. In a school, certain criteria determine what level each student will pursue, and certain skills will determine how much mastery and efficiency a student has. In this school of love, sometimes we are excelling by leaps and bounds, but sometimes we are stagnant. At times, we even go backwards and get demoted. The material body and material world is comparable to a reformatory or a prison. *To the degree that we focus on the body, we change the school of love into a prison.*

These reflections should help us understand why we sometimes feel enthusiasm in our lives that is substantive and spiritual, and why at other times we feel emptiness. Why, at times, does the whole universe seem to choke us; our service seem to beat us; our relationships seem to disappoint us; or our job—or lack of a job—seem to frustrate us? For many people, just getting up in the morning involves trauma and pain because they have forgotten that they are made for love. Many people fail in this school because they are somehow waiting for the lesson and waiting for the opportunity without realizing that the lesson and the chance to excel is always available. People who are waiting to be loved before they can give love will constantly be waiting.

Any type of relationship we have provides an opportunity to share love. While relating to those who might have a superior position such as parents or teachers, we can exchange love by receiving advice and wisdom. With our peers, we can always share some kind of healthy communication, service, and friendship. With those who might not be as experienced as ourselves or younger in the school, we can always share some sense of love by trying to guide and facilitate them in different ways. When we share love among all these different levels of associates, it becomes more difficult for us to forget who we are, and we have a greater chance of becoming certified in this school. If a person can learn from younger students, from his or her peers, and from those in higher grades, that individual will become a very progressive student. Certainly that student will also become an excellent teacher since they will have so much to share due to their alertness in the school.

The teachers are there to direct, guide, and show love. For instance, every so often special entities come into the school or into this material world to see who is ready to graduate into the land of ultimate, animated love. These are the great prophets, teachers, and *acaryas*. Sometimes they act as bounty hunters who go looking for those who are ready to return to the pure land of love. When such bounty hunters go into the different environments, most entities who have forgotten their real identity run from these helpers. They run from those personalities who have actually come to help them regain what they have temporarily lost. They run into all types of situations that help them propagate the illusion that they are not loved and that they have no love to share.

However, we want to take their help because they can help us acquire the proper qualifications to graduate from this school. We want their help so that we can avoid selfishness. We do not just want to be selfish students, trying to see what we can get; rather, we want to advance so that we can teach and facilitate others while simultaneously trying to graduate ourselves. Furthermore, as we become teachers, we will become more absorbed in chances to share love. And as we share, we want to become more astute at receiving so that we have more to share. What is worse than having a teacher who gives the same lesson every single semester? Not only will the teacher become bored with the subject matter, but the teacher will also bore the students because he or she will just give a mechanical performance. Most teachers function in this way. They know the lesson plan which they have mastered to a certain extent, and therefore they just speak mechanically. Not only are they bored, but they also bore their students. And the students just want their degrees so that they can graduate and start earning money. They minimize the point of the lessons and the experience. We also find this problem in spiritual circles.

Genuine Teachers Can Enthuse Their Students

There are so many teachers who know the philosophy and theology, but since they have not truly imbibed the teaching, they cannot enthuse people deep in their hearts. Remember that in the school of love, we cannot cheat. In material schools, some people might be able to cram at the last minute or even pass tests without learning or experiencing the material. They simply give the teacher what he or she wants. Teachers who only want the material regurgitated back in a specific way without the pupil accessing the essence are cheaters. Their students will learn nothing more than mastering this cheating propensity.

Many people graduate from this type of school as expert cheaters. They have learned the science of how to study, but understand very little while pretending to know so much. They can pass all the quizzes and tests in such a way that it seems as if they have taken the subject matter very seriously. Of course, this can only happen when students have cheating teachers because cheating teachers will honor cheating students. However, when a teacher is genuine, the students cannot get away with cheating in this way. A proper teacher will expose the student's level of understanding so that the student can learn the material properly. But the teacher has to be absorbed in love to recognize and stimulate love in others.

For this reason, we cannot cheat in the school of love. In

a regular academic school, one student might seem to work very hard and even get a good grade although he or she did not use all of his or her skills. In another case, a student might not perform as nicely externally and might not receive a high grade, but the individual put forth greater effort and used all of his or her skills. The teacher who is only looking for external productivity may quickly give the first student a high grade and the second student a low grade without considering any other factors. However, many teachers understand that one student's "A" might be of a higher quality than another student's "A" because one student put more effort into the work than the other. One student really imbibed the essence of the course. Someone might be more intelligent and pass the course easily, but the material will not have much meaning to them later in life. Another student might struggle more to get a good grade, but he or she has really imbibed the subject matter. In spirituality, these factors are essential.

    The Lord looks at our capacity and our ability. He understands all of our limitations and judges us according to how we genuinely use what we have. This school of love is wonderful. In the material world, we must constantly confront different assaults, but the school of love can remind us of our higher purpose. Even if we seemingly do not have enough money, health, or support, we can realize that ultimately it does not matter because the spiritual warrior knows that nothing can stop God's love. And nothing can stop our chance to also be as loving as possible. *Every moment is a chance to give and receive more love.*

The Correlation between Love and Happiness

In order to access our humanity and spirituality, we must accept our loving nature and our ability to impact upon others lovingly. If we had a barometer that could determine our level of happiness and fulfillment in life, it would correspond directly to how much we function as carriers of love. For instance, if we accept our constitutional position as loving beings, no lack of material facility could stop us from sharing that love. It just means that we would have a different arena in which to experience who we are and to share what we have. *If we accept that we are really made for love, it does not matter what kinds of complications come upon us. We will just see them as opportunities to capture love and give love.* Whenever we come across an opportunity, we want it to help us find a way to exchange love. We will perceive all activities and emotions as an exchange of love or as a cry for love.

We can see anxiety in different ways. Some people have so much to do and others have nothing to do. Those who have opportunities to do many things are in anxiety because they are overwhelmed with the dilemma of how to accomplish all of their tasks. On the other hand, those who don't have any challenges in their lives are overwhelmed with the anxiety and frustration of boredom. Those who have children are overwhelmed with the responsibilities that parenthood brings. Those who don't have children are sometimes overwhelmed due to their desire to take care of such entities. Those who have a spouse are sometimes overwhelmed since that spouse does not always act according to their expectations. Those who don't have a spouse are sometimes overwhelmed because they don't have a relationship. However, if we accept that we are in the school of love, such anxieties will stem from wonderful chances to engage in the process of *sadhana-bhakti* or spiritual practices. We will want to absorb our mind and senses in whatever field of activity we find ourselves in, and we will want to offer that to the Lord.

As we recognize more and more that we are made for love, then as we sweep the floor, wash the dishes, clean the yard, or take care of our cars, we will experience a certain happiness because we will perform all of these activities with loving care. If we forget that we are made for love, then all of these basic activities that are a part of "normal" life will be painful. We will not recognize an opportunity to give and receive love through the performance of these duties. As we try to maintain our finances, take care of our health, or perform our religious practices, we will find many chances to love ourselves—our true selves. We actually have many chances to say yes to God's love. As we say our prayers, engage in meditation, chant, etc., we have a chance to intensify the visions of love. It is a reality that as we go deeper and deeper in our spiritual growth, the music becomes sweeter and the meditations on our home in the spiritual world—the abode of unconditional love—become more prominent in our lives. Living this way turns into a natural way of life. As we reflect with purity, we begin to experience connections with the spiritual realm. But this will happen only as we increasingly see our environment as a catalyst for different expressions of love.

Most people try to find deep fulfillment in matter. Some are trying to find it in another individual, which obviously leads to difficulty. To think that one person can help us experience our total fullness in love is to be a covered atheist. People who do this are essentially thinking that another person can function as their God. Ultimately, we want to enter into relationships with the idea that another person can help remind us about the

Lord and we can remind them about the Lord due to a high level of love. We should pursue this high level of interaction with our husband or wife, our friends, our children, and even in our relationships at work. As long as we are not involved in a sinful activity, even our jobs or services should be opportunities to become more absorbed in the school of love and in its rewards.

Useless Substitutes for Love

Look at the degree of happiness, excitement, activity, and security in our lives. If these qualities do not fill our lives, we might find that we are actually overwhelmed by their opposites. The converse of happiness is sadness. We have happiness in this school of love to the degree that we are honoring who we are, and the sadness is connected with our forgetfulness. The converse of excitement is boredom. When we are bored, we think there are no chances to give love; therefore, we become dry and dull. We fail to see all the opportunities manifesting around us. The converse of activity is too much inactivity. It means that we are minimizing opportunities, denying them, or seeing them as botherations. Look at security versus insecurity. When we feel secure, we are thinking that we are in the right place at the right time and we feel protected. Insecurity leads to opposing feelings such as confusion or fear. We do not feel that our circumstances are meant for our growth. This type of mentality is covered atheism because we are forgetting that the Lord has arranged things even though we may not always understand the reason. The Lord does not go on vacation, neglect us, or have favorites. He always deeply loves every soul and arranges challenges and adventures for each of us.

Introduction: The School of Love

Relying on substitutes for love means we are not hungry enough yet. The hunger is there, but we are trying to fill it with inadequate substitutes. This will not work. If the tank of your car is empty, you cannot expect it to run just by pouring water in that tank. The water will fill the tank, but the car will not run. Similarly, we cannot expect to be happy in our spiritual lives by filling ourselves with things that do not honor our actual purpose and identity. However, if we remind ourselves that we are made for love and are loved deeply, then we can again feel happy, excited, active, and secure while we wait for additional understanding and support. Regardless of our circumstances, there are always many ways to experience and give love.

Imagine people trying to find that love in a relative or temporary way, which we normally understand as lust. They will confront many stumbling blocks and not excel in this school. And after awhile, what happens? When someone is taking a course in school but cannot seem to grasp the subject matter, after awhile they give up and might even want to leave school completely. People pursuing various activities and religious paths will also abandon their goals if they somehow do not accelerate and make progress. They will leave the institution or the course. They will run away from that which could help them become totally liberated and free.

We need to remember that every day is a chance to study a lesson and pass a test. Every day is a chance to associate with others. But we have to determine the quality of that association because it impacts the quality of our studying. Sometimes the worst association is our mind. It tells us, "You are a failure. You can't pass this lesson. You are useless, worthless, and unworthy of love." Even though we are inherently meant for love, the mind tricks us in these unfortunate ways, dragging us away from our constitutional position.

So much of life is becoming more exciting because I am beginning to fall in love with everyone I deal with, and I can see how refreshing and energizing such exchanges can be. I don't care who it is because everyone is distinctly an aspect of the Lord, part and parcel of the same Godhead. In each relationship, we can experience a deep quality of existence as we try to share something, regardless of how small. Just consider that the person is made for love, you are made for love, and the ultimate lover is Mother-Father God. Relationships in their fullest expression are God-centered and in connection with love, which minimizes the chance of setbacks or ongoing anxieties.

We Cannot Cheat

In order to grow properly in this school of love, we must become free of *bhukti*, *mukti*, and *siddhi*, or the desires for sense enjoyment, liberation, and mystic powers. We must become free of unhealthy attachments to matter. We must stop trying to experience the energy of the Lord through impersonal alignments because our most beloved Lord is ready to give personally if we approach Him genuinely. He is ready even more than we could ever consider. However, if we still want to somehow push the beloved out of the way to reach our superficial goals, it simply will not work. The beauty of the school of love is that cheating will not work.

Anyone who tries to cheat takes away from their own credit and growth. There is no cheating—only deposits and withdrawals. When we think that we are successfully cheating, the monitors of the school of love are noting withdrawals from our bank account. When we think that we are getting away with some deviation or lack of intensity, we are ruining our position as good students. Conversely, when we engage in practicing devotional service to God, we are making deposits into our bank account. The health of our spiritual bank account determines how fast we become certified as pure lovers. Certification means no more tests but only steady performances. When we inhabit a material body in the material world, there will be constant tests, and tests are challenges that you can either pass or fail. Once we have understood the lesson and passed the test, it becomes a matter of performance and of acting upon what we have practiced. Actually, all of our so-called relationships of love here on this plane are really to help us fix whatever has to be fixed before we enter into the spiritual world of divine, eternal romance.

Dependence on the Lord

For this reason, the Lord tells us to always think of Him. The essence of all Vedic teachings is to always think of the Lord and never forget Him. Always thinking of our beloved with genuine love brings amazing solace. And if we truly experience deep love, forgetting the beloved who we deeply think about and care for is minimizing our own existence. It is like death. And to not be able to reciprocate with our beloved is also another expression of death, especially since we are made for love.

In this school of love, the svarupa-laksana or our most essential asset is full dependence on the Lord. We want to always remember our most beloved Lord and never forget Him. We want to do that which is favorable for devotional service and reject anything that impedes our remembrance of

Him. We want to do anything that will allow His love to come through and avoid anything that prevents the love from coming through.

Each of us can determine how fast or slow that experience of deep love comes upon us based on whether we are constantly depositing or constantly withdrawing. For many people, it takes lifetimes to experience the deep love because they deposit and then withdraw and withdraw and withdraw. After awhile, they might even be expelled from the school for a period of time. Stagnancy is dangerous because it can cause us to want to enter into another school. Let us pray to the highest community of love—the spiritual abode—and let us constantly access the activities and consciousness that enhance that love. As we have all our other duties, concerns, and problems, let us see them as opportunities to give and receive more love. This becomes natural as we transform lust into love.

Chapter 1

Sex and the Leadership Crisis

As we enter the twenty-first century, the world faces innumerable challenges. Although technological advancements have succeeded in making some inhabitants of this planet more comfortable, in general people do not seem to be happier or more peaceful. Huge inequities continue to exist around the globe, and even among the affluent, material prosperity does not guarantee fulfillment. The planet's ecosystems are seriously out of balance; wars and conflicts exact a tragic toll; and all around us people are pursuing prestige and profit at almost any price.

What is the reason for such a state of affairs? To find an answer, we must look beyond the surface of events and probe deeply into our own hearts. The ultimate cause is not a specific set of historical events—important though these may be—but our own thoughts, feelings, and desires. As members of modern industrial culture, we can hardly keep from imbibing its messages. Consequently, most of us have learned to view ourselves as physical beings that "only go around once," and we accept the pursuit of sense gratification as normal. As a corollary, we have permitted ourselves to indulge our many material appetites, which we seek to satisfy by any number of means.

Another way to describe our situation is to say that we have allowed lust, rather than love, to govern our lives. Despite our best intentions, this society makes it difficult to avoid living in a self-centered, competitive, exploitive way. Lust encourages us to continue our wanton exploitation of the Earth's resources in a never-ending cycle so that we can produce more, consume more, profit more, and want more. Lust makes us climb the ladder of "success" to the top without regard for the harm we may cause along the way. And lust makes us indulge in sexual behavior that hurts and degrades others and ourselves. To make a change for the better, we must learn how to transform our lust into love. The future of the world depends on it.

Lust, Sex, and Leadership

Nowhere is the need for this transformation of lust into love more apparent than among our leaders. *One of the greatest problems in the world today is the impotence of our leaders at all levels of society.* In general, they have been unable, or unwilling, to conquer their lust. In particular, they have not learned how to use sexual energies in a constructive way and so cannot master the self-serving attachments that stand in the way of a more selfless, spiritual expression of love.[1]

As the eighteenth-century French writer, Voltaire, once said, the masses are docile. They are susceptible to fads and trends, and they emulate those who lead them. That is why the inadequacy of leaders poses such a serious problem. The entire planet follows in their footsteps. Our leaders are insufficiently equipped to confront the negative currents that are so prevalent today, and they cannot summon intervention from higher spiritual levels to uplift the general consciousness of society. Because of these weaknesses, everyone is increasingly at the mercy of demonic energies.

Misused Sexuality Is the Cause

Sexuality is a powerful force that we can use in constructive or destructive ways. Although sexual energy can build up civilizations or tear them down, our leaders still do not recognize the need to master its many forms. Despite the fact that people constantly hear about sex, talk about it, think about it, and engage in it, they are ignorant of its more profound aspects. Yet a proper comprehension of sexuality is essential not only for personal evolution, but also for strong nation building.

Many seemingly powerful leaders have ultimately failed in their respective missions because of an inability to control their sexual energy. Misdirected sexuality has caused countless political regimes to crumble and has torn asunder innumerable religious and spiritual institutions. Millions of people have even lost their lives because of leaders who fell prey to poorly channeled sexual energies. Indeed, the patriarchal nature of society itself encourages a wide variety of self-indulgent boundary violations, so that today's culture is replete with signs of sexual imbalance: pornography, promiscuity, abortion, incest, bestiality, and sexually transmitted diseases.

Society Encourages Sense Gratification

Sex in itself is not harmful; indeed, quite the opposite is the case. We are not trying to devalue sexuality in any way, but are instead questioning the approach modern society takes to it. When sex is an expression of love, it can become a great positive force that yields many deep spiritual revelations and realizations. At its highest level, sexuality becomes a tremendous service to God and to the planet. In the *Bhagavad-gita* 7.11, an ancient Vedic text, the Lord says, *dharmaviruddho bhutesu kamo 'smi bharatarsabha*: "I am sex life which is not contrary to religious principles."

Materialistic civilization has confused love with sex. It is no surprise that someone is raped almost every minute in the United States or that about one-sixth of all children, boys as well as girls, have been victims of incest. We are constantly bombarded by advertisements urging us to enjoy our senses. Whether the product is a candy bar, a beverage, or a car, the idea behind each advertisement is that the consumer takes possession, enjoys, and thereby increases the potential for an exciting sex life.

A major contributing factor to our difficulty in controlling sexual appetites is the influence of television and other media. Anyone who watches a few hours of television each day cannot help becoming sexually agitated. Not only do advertisements have sexual overtones, but most of the programs do as well. Movies are especially preoccupied with sex. This might not be a problem if the films portrayed healthy relationships, but unfortunately they often show exploitation, abuse, and perversion. People also spend amazing amounts of money for special "adult" videos, or for sexual programming via cable. And what do they think their children are watching when they turn on the television?

Television puts us in an alpha state, similar to hypnosis, which makes us far more receptive to suggestion than usual. As we watch, images implant themselves in our minds, where they can linger for days, weeks, months, or even years. Think about it. Remember the last time you saw an intensely sexual scene, and recall how long it remained with you. With such images in our consciousness, no wonder we have such great difficulty resisting the temptations of promiscuity.

This situation is no accident. Whenever we misuse a powerful constructive force such as sexual energy, that same force can become equally strong in a negative way. In this society, many are deliberately trying to encourage our dependence upon sex and drugs for their personal gain. Because we have not learned to master our sexual energies, we are easy prey, becoming enslaved to our senses and, by extension, to those who profit from our weaknesses. This is why the illicit drug and pharmaceutical trade is the largest business in the world, and why pornography is one of this planet's greatest growth industries.

Consequences of Misdirected Sexual Energy

Pornography is often connected with organized crime and its harmful activities. The influence of pornography can increase the incidence of rape and destroy healthy relationships, breaking up families and discouraging meaningful connections with others. Because pornography is so prevalent, people begin to emulate the degradation they see, accepting such perversions as normal and justifying all kinds of reprehensible behavior.

In addition to pornography, another negative consequence of misused sexual energy is the rapid spread of sexually transmitted diseases around the planet. Each year, millions of new cases of syphilis and gonorrhea appear, and every day several thousand people become infected with the AIDS virus, so that in the next few years untold millions will fall ill.

We will remain vulnerable to sexual exploitation and to the temptation of drugs until we find a higher purpose for our lives. A greater understanding of life's spiritual meaning will ultimately allow us to develop more compassion and selflessness, using the great restorative power of our sexual energies to love and care for others instead of directing them toward destructive ends.

Bisexuality and Homosexuality

Another manifestation of the role of sexuality in modern society is homosexuality and the growing number of bisexuals around the world. Of course, we should not be homophobic, nor should we condemn anyone for the choices they make. Everyone is simply looking for love. However, many people, gay or straight, are just avoiding an honest, hopefully spiritual, monogamous relationship. Such people are guided by selfish lust rather than accountable, selfless, and compassionate love. Many straight people are quick to lump all gay people together which is just as absurd as viewing all straight people to be the same. There are many varieties of gay people whose consciousness can vary from the most mundane to the most highly spiritual, just as in the heterosexual community.

One of the Vedic texts, the *Kama-sutra*, includes gay people in the categories of *tritiya-prakriti* or the "third sex." A certain, renounced class of these individuals lived in their own villages, practiced celibacy, and were invited to attend or perform at important gatherings or festivals, and their presence was considered very auspicious. "...That is their means of livelihood. Such men never become servants or engage themselves in agriculture or business occupations; they simply take charity from neighborhood friends to maintain themselves peacefully" (*Caitanya-caritamrta Adi-lila* 13.106 purport).

Obtaining the body of a man, a woman, or of the third gender is a choice, but not necessarily a choice made in this lifetime. Everyone who has a material body is a product of *karma* from a previous lifetime, which involves their choices, experiences, and desires. All of these factors add up directly and indirectly, producing not only our particular bodies but also our psyche, relationships, and field of activities in each incarnation. Some people are born with very unusual configurations of chromosomes or with complex and mixed genital structures. Thus, they come into the world with a certain physical proclivity. Such people as well as all people in general have had their mentality impacted upon by previous experiences in past lives and by critical periods in this lifetime.

Regardless of our hormonal and chromosomal configurations, and our psychological and emotional states, we all have the same choice in this lifetime—to use our body, senses, and mind in love and service to God, or to use them for lust and exploitation. Let us examine a few possible sociological and metaphysical factors that can also play a role in transgender behavior.

For many gay males, a factor is their desire to avoid imitating the male role models they witnessed as children. If a boy sees his father showing disrespect for his mother and refusing to support his own children, will he be proud to become a man? When a boy sees his mother crying because her husband has abandoned the family, will that child be eager to become like his father?

Most modern cultures are founded upon an autocratic, patriarchal model of human interaction. The normal behavior of males in these systems is to be lords of everything they survey. Such societies encourage men to be ruthless, self-centered, manipulative dictators, despite the wish of many to be kind, compassionate protectors and providers. Men who do not have a wholesome respect for themselves can easily succumb to these social pressures by fully embracing "macho" behavior—or totally rejecting it.

Even women have internalized this patriarchal pattern; many of them are only too eager to take advantage of others, male and female, for their own personal gain. Regardless of gender, anyone in a position of seniority who lacks love and compassion inevitably becomes an exploiter. Such exploitation perpetuates the patriarchal paradigm that continues to hurt so many of us.

Females face so many unnecessary challenges. Many young girls experience abuse and mistreatment just because they are female. The patriarchal culture teaches a young woman not to value her femininity. A woman walking down a street must be vigilant just because she is female. She must be cautious even when greeting or smiling at a man, because he may misinterpret her behavior. She has to be wary when her boss makes certain comments, because he may have another meaning in mind. She may work hard at her job only to discover that she is paid far less than a man doing the same work. Under such a relentless onslaught, how can anyone be happy about being female?

Spiritual Aspects of Homosexuality

From a spiritual perspective, another explanation for homosexuality or bisexuality can lie in reincarnation. Those who are not properly integrated in one life could have in the next life a male consciousness in a female body, or vice versa. Such souls are stuck, just like anyone who has a material body. The situation is not completely their doing, because many people have participated in creating the environment and culture that have allowed such circumstances to develop. In many cases, if a person has demonstrated excessive masculine or feminine energy in one life, or strong hatred for one sex or the other, these patterns can persist in the next life—even in a body of the opposite gender. This can encourage a homosexual lifestyle.

Remember, this whole world is designed as a training ground or school. A soul in a previous life may have been in a strong, athletic, 250-pound male weight-lifter's body. Now this soul is reborn in a woman's body. As a man, perhaps this individual was extremely chauvinistic, insensitive, and unwilling to develop his nurturing side. He must now take on a female identity in order to develop these aspects. But his strong connection to his previous life means that he still expresses powerful masculine energy, so that now the person is in a state of bewilderment. This soul may have to reincarnate in the next life as a woman once again in order to integrate the denied feminine aspects.

As another example, in a previous life, someone in a female body may have experienced extreme abuse. Now that same individual is born once again in a female body, this time filled with great self-hatred and dislike of being female. In an effort to deny her hated femininity, she creates an imbalance in her sexual orientation.

If a person feels attraction toward members of their own sex, they are not alone. Great numbers of people have similar karmic factors to work out. There is nothing wrong with having affection for someone of the same gender. However, the difficulties arise when this affection seeks illicit sexual expression. Sex life means that the partners are ready to care for what is produced from their union. What can naturally result from a sexual relationship is the birth of a child. Any other use of sexuality can be unnatural, and can entail inauspicious consequences.

Other Esoteric Aspects of Sexuality

From a spiritual viewpoint, not only does reincarnation play a role in homosexuality, but it can also explain the attraction we may experience for certain members of the opposite sex. We have all lived many lifetimes, during which we have certainly engaged in sexual activity. In this present life we may meet a sexual partner from a previous existence for whom we feel overwhelming desire, without understanding why. Actually, we are experiencing the subtle connection that exists because we have shared so much from the past.

But now there is a problem. That person may be our best friend's wife or husband, or our own son or daughter. Can you understand how difficult such a situation may be? Those involved are pulled in conflicting directions by forces beyond their comprehension. The remedy is to live in such a principle-centered way that, even though these attractions exist, we do not act upon them. If we indulge ourselves, chaos will result.

There is another reason spiritual people may feel strong sexual attraction in inappropriate circumstances. Sometimes souls awaiting birth need a special type of earthly environment to develop properly, especially those who want a special body or upbringing to support higher consciousness. Such souls will seek a particular pair of human beings—not necessarily married to each other—who can provide the necessary biology, protection, guidance, or training for them after they come into this world.

These souls will put pressure on the consciousness of the selected couple whenever those two people are together, regardless of marriage commitments to other partners or religious vows of celibacy. The external situation is irrelevant to these souls, who are simply focused upon their goal.

This in no way excuses someone who breaks religious or marital vows, but it does explain an unacknowledged source of the overwhelming sexual attraction that sometimes arises between people—often in spiritual groups. *Because our society so frequently confuses love with sex,* even people on a spiritual path may be tempted to lust after their associates just like anyone else. Although they may think they have found their "soul mates," they may simply be sexually attracted or subject to pressures from souls seeking to take birth in a good body or to grow up in a supportive environment.

How to Remedy the Situation

Due to their special responsibilities and vulnerabilities, spiritual leaders in particular must be careful not to act upon the strong sexual stimulation they may feel on occasion. They must maintain their mastery of the senses if they do not want to risk destroying their organizations and the faith of many people.

Attractions will naturally arise. We should not feel ashamed or embarrassed by them, but we must learn how to handle the feelings in a way that does not cause disturbance. If the persons selected as potential parents do not understand what is happening, or if they do not remain firm in their vows, they may become overwhelmed by sexual desire and succumb. Targeted people must be alert to these situations and learn to communicate subtly with souls seeking birth, explaining to them the unsuitability of the circumstances.

Another course of action is to ask the demigods to direct these particular souls to other, more appropriate environments. The demigods help in making the first decisions regarding where such souls will be placed. Many people may believe that the demigods do not really exist and are just theoretical, but actually the universe is highly personal. The demigods control all of our bodily functions—the blinking of our eyes, our respiration, or our elimination, for example—and they are extremely active on this planet. They can and do help.

If a soul is trying to provoke a married woman to have an affair, the demigods could direct that soul to become the child of the woman and her legitimate husband. As another option, a soul who is trying to tempt a priest could take birth in a family close to the priest, who might then help raise the child. A case in point comes from my own experience. I am celibate and therefore do not engage in sex life. Frequently, souls who have or seek a connection with me appear in families of my disciples so that I can care for them.

Most spiritual and secular leaders have no understanding of such phenomena. But that does not matter. The remedy is the same whether we understand what is happening or not. We must control the senses, remain principle-centered, and develop contact with spiritual mentors who can help us remain strong. If we persist in using our power to exploit or abuse others, we will suffer the consequences. Higher spiritual beings are always monitoring us and holding us accountable for our behavior. They are constantly concerned about us, watching us, thinking about us, and wanting to help. This is all done out of deep love for us. God and His agents love us all and therefore arrange many ways to guide and assist us.

Subtle Sex

The influence of sexuality is far more pervasive than we may think. One poorly understood aspect of sexuality is a phenomenon called subtle sex. Even if we refrain from overt sexual activity, we may still seek to dominate our environment, either by trying to control everything and everyone around us or by letting others know how wonderful and important we are. When we devote our energies to acquiring excessive distinction, adoration, and self-centered profit, we are engaging in forms of subtle sex. Such behavior is considered normal in materialistic society; therefore it can be extremely difficult to remain immune to its attractions.

The pursuit of excessive distinction, adoration, and profit is a symptom pointing to a lack of mastery over sexual energy. Unchecked, our egocentric desires can degrade into overt physical activities. Whenever we are focused on our own sovereign pleasure in the form of prestige, power, and personal gain, we tend to exploit others, seeing them as extensions of ourselves and using them for our own selfish gratification.

When powerful leaders succumb to the desire for distinction, there is no doubt about what is happening behind closed doors. Since such individuals are already out of order, they lack the discipline to refrain from sexual indulgence. In contrast, genuinely strong leaders—Mahatma Gandhi, the Dalai Lama, or Mother Teresa, for example—did not behave in this way. Instead, they based their strength on selflessness and humility.

Such leaders develop spiritual armor that protects them from the attractions and dangers of subtle sex.

Sexual Energy and Peace

World peace is not possible until we master our sexual energies, including our propensities to indulge in subtle sex. Peace ultimately depends upon developing better relationships within our own families and with the people we encounter every day. To improve these relationships we must find peace within ourselves. Inner peace means discovering our internal balance, which leads us directly back to the issue of developing proper control and regulation of our sexual energies. If we do not learn how to channel and integrate these energies properly, we have little chance of creating a peaceful world.

Once we have learned to live harmoniously with ourselves, relationships with other people, especially family members, automatically improve. In turn, this improvement has a positive effect upon our communities and our nations, and eventually upon the entire global community. Remember, the world's current lack of harmony is largely a result of our failure to express love instead of seeking sense gratification. That is why it is essential to free ourselves from the clutches of lust and channel our sexual energies more constructively.

The Power of Sexual Energy

If we examine the sexual practices of many other species on the planet, we can gain an even greater understanding of the power of sexual energy. In some cases, the sex act itself is so significant that a member of a species has only one chance to perform it. For example, the male butterfly mates once and then dies. The female lays hundreds of eggs and then her life is over too. Ants and certain spiders also have only one opportunity to procreate. In these species, the sexual act is so powerful that it ends physical life.

In the human species, as we have seen, sexuality can be a constructive or destructive force, depending upon one's level of consciousness. All spiritual traditions acknowledge the power of sexuality, teaching us how to control and channel it in order to attain deeper communion with the Divine. At the same time, improper use of this same energy has driven some to commit vicious atrocities. Amidst the turbulence of today's world, we must choose how we will direct our sexual energies. We can either develop the energy in a positive direction or focus on gratifying our selfish desires, thereby contributing to a general decline that could eventually destroy our culture and even the entire planet.

An Unfortunate Example

Many years ago, President Kaunda of Zambia—also Chairman of the Organization of African Unity (OAU) at the time—hosted a vegetarian banquet in my honor. Members of his central committee were invited, along with my staff. Most members of his inner circle were Marxists, and they noticed with dismay that the President was strongly attracted to what I was saying. A few of them began to take issue with me.

I was discussing deep spiritual principles as well as social issues, describing alternative schools and farms, and proposing remedies for problems such as the illicit drug trade. The members of the central committee explained that many missionaries had come to Zambia in the name of religion and caused great harm, offering the Bible in one hand and taking land with the other. They were afraid that I might be playing the same game or that I might be a CIA agent.

Their ultimate question was, "How do we know that you walk your talk? How can we be sure that you are truly on the side of the people?" I realized that these men were speaking from genuine concern. But I also knew that their country had a serious problem with drugs, and that many of the men talking to me were directly responsible for it. Strangely, they seemed genuinely unaware of their own hypocrisy.

I pointed out this inconsistency, saying, "You claim to be concerned about the people, talking about revolution and raising consciousness, but basically everything about your lifestyle is degrading and debilitating. This negativity is what you are emanating to your country. You cannot be a proper caretaker of others unless you live a disciplined life. Whenever you lack sense control, adverse factions will attack you and encourage you to give in to your weakness." Such self-indulgent behavior has been accepted in that country—and many others—for generations.

I began to elaborate, "You are chain smokers. You are meat-eaters, taking abominable things into your bodies. You have sex with almost anything that moves. And yet you talk about your concern for the people, all the while exploiting them directly by your schemes, and undermining them indirectly by your examples. You are guiding them toward destruction!"

To conclude, I emphasized once again the importance of sense control, explaining that leaders who have a genuine spiritual connection are far greater revolutionaries than the communists. The commitment of such leaders to the people enables them to forgo their own immediate pleasures for a higher level of activity that benefits everyone.

Abuses of Power

Although this discussion with President Kaunda and his aides took place many years ago, the theme is as fresh today as it was then. In a world where promiscuity is undermining relationships, incest is destroying families, and greed is hampering the productivity of corporations, most leaders lack the self-discipline to properly support their constituents.

Those in power can raise consciousness to support a positive global mind shift, or they can do the opposite. The outcome depends largely upon the extent to which they can control their sexual energies, particularly in stressful situations. When leaders—just like any of us—experience misfortunes such as divorce, unemployment, disease, or death of a loved one, others may seek to capitalize on their vulnerability. Leaders must be strictly vigilant at such times, both in seeking help and in offering it to someone else. Compromising situations can arise unexpectedly. They are not always consciously planned, but can occur because those involved do not understand the forces at work and the severity of the consequences.

Leaders who take advantage of others are contributing to the decline of our society instead of serving as our protectors and role models. When they engage in sexual exploitation, do they realize that they are hurting somebody's mother, sister, daughter, wife, or fiancée? Do they understand the harm they are doing to themselves and their own families? They are encouraging a lifestyle that completely misuses the sexual energies and destroys people, organizations, and ultimately entire societies.

Whether they are clergy, CEOs, military officers, teachers, therapists, politicians, bosses, or parents, leaders must accept the responsibility inherent in having power over others, especially at this time in history when many people are deeply needy. We should recognize that abusing those who place their trust in us brings serious consequences.

Secular and spiritual leaders today who lack control over their sexual energies have greatly damaged, or even destroyed, their nations or organizations. Conditions of degradation that many of us accept as normal—in our cities, businesses, governments, families, and spiritual organizations—are consequences of such perverted leadership. Some political leaders have murdered countless numbers of people or created conditions in which human survival becomes difficult, if not impossible. Still others have caused such profound disillusionment that individuals have taken their own lives.

These issues touch us all. Everyone is a leader in one way or another, and everyone has contact with leaders. Due to the examples they set and the power they wield, leaders must control their senses, regulate their sexual energy, and conquer any desire to control and exploit others. Responsible leaders are not slaves to their passions and more urgently than anyone else, they must live a strict life.

The Proper Role of Leaders

In our social groups, political institutions, schools, places of work, spiritual organizations, and homes, leaders must create an ethical and constructive climate for all concerned, constantly monitoring their behavior and that of others. To become positive forces on this planet, they must learn to give expression to the wisdom of the soul and lead us all to a higher plane.

Ideally, all leaders should serve as representatives of God, promoting the physical, mental, emotional, and spiritual well-being of others without desire for personal gain. Spiritual leadership in particular entails special responsibilities, because those who care for others spiritually have the express mandate to love, guide, and protect. Their activities are meant to bring blessings to the entire community because they are empowered to elevate consciousness and to convey mercy. Their caretaking role automatically wins the trust of others; in a sense such leaders are the spiritual parents of those in their charge. Sexual exploitation, always reprehensible, is a particularly deplorable betrayal in this context.

In ancient times, communities expected their political leaders to have a spiritual connection. A society did not choose a king who was merely a good warrior or politician, but one who also understood the science of caring for the people and who could communicate with higher spiritual realms. Righteous kingmakers or priests would monitor such leaders to ensure proper behavior. But today, cheaters and the cheated surround us, and everyone is running after sense gratification.

Because *all* leaders—not just spiritual leaders—serve as representatives of God, the actions of those who take unfair advantage of others can have enormous impact. In our families, for example, parents should be channeling divine energies to their children. Unfortunately, all too often this does not happen. The amount of incest all over the planet is frightening, and appalling numbers of people suffer the aftereffects of other forms of sexual abuse as well. Many individuals cannot have healthy sexual relationships, recoiling in fear from another's touch, experiencing terrible migraine headaches, or wetting the bed even as adults. In some cases such people can never lead normal lives, because those whom they trusted and loved betrayed and exploited them. Imagine the depth of the wounds when parents betray their children in such a way, and the terrible hurt and disillusionment when spiritual leaders engage in such deviant activities. They leave marks that will last, in some cases, for generations.

Leaders should never consider themselves as proprietors of those in their charge. Ownership implies that we have the right to do with our property as we will, and it can serve as a justification for all kinds of exploitation and abuse. But if we view ourselves as caretakers, coordinators, catalysts, or carriers of the vision, and if we treat others in loving, supportive ways, we will not engage in such exploitation.

The Importance of Boundaries

If we are to be effective spiritual leaders, we must respect the boundaries of others. Yet this respect must not go to unhealthy extremes. In contemporary society, which lacks spiritual culture and considers everything to be relative, people claim their own truth, saying, "I have my truth, so let me do my own thing." Ultimately, this means that there is no truth; there is only anarchy. Those who cling to their so-called truth can easily use their own idiosyncratic desires and tendencies to abuse and exploit others.

Healthy, constructive boundaries allow people enough room to grow and serve God in their own individual ways, without interference. At the same time, effective boundaries recognize the importance of spiritual guidelines to help society develop properly in alignment with divine principles. *A wise leader treads a fine line, neither violating the rights of others nor allowing anarchy to reign.*

Boundaries are also important for leaders themselves to help maintain their integrity and balance. If we are constantly bombarded by energies from our surroundings without developing inner strength, eventually we become drained, lonely, and empty. Then the first impulse that comes to many of us is to fill the void through sex.

No one can be a leader, with all the intensity that implies, without regular rest and renewal. Those serving as spiritual mentors in particular provide strength, protection, and guidance to people seeking help, and many powerful psychic contacts take place. Such leaders require a generous amount of psychological space in order to restore their energies and contact their inner wisdom. Without it, after a while the urgent needs, demands, and dependencies of others can begin to affect their consciousness.

Spiritual leaders who do not rejuvenate themselves and fail to constantly strengthen their internal resources can become great embarrassments to their own traditions. Instead of being helpful, they may then begin to perceive themselves as superior, believing that everything originates with them and that they should be amply rewarded. When this occurs, they are well on their way to becoming enormous hindrances to spiritual progress. In contrast, spiritual leaders who are properly aligned and balanced can make a positive contribution to the world.

This Is War

How do leaders—or any of us—become properly aligned and balanced? In order to answer this question, we must gain a deeper understanding of the various manifestations of lust and love. The remaining chapters of this book address these topics at length, revealing the forces acting within us and around us that can be directed either toward saving the world or destroying it.

Make no mistake. This is a time of warfare against the dark forces. All of us, and leaders in particular, require spiritual weapons for survival. *Proper use of sexual energy is an essential ingredient for making a positive shift in consciousness on this planet.* We must become strong and stand firm, because the negative influences are rapidly increasing, especially against those who are seeking higher consciousness. We must fortify ourselves by learning to live on a higher level, where we have more permanent and substantive lasting relationships—genuine unions based on deep love. That is what this book is about.

Questions and Answers

Question: You have described so many ways in which we are affected by lust and negative expressions of sexuality. How can we develop pure love for others?

Answer: It is not as hard as it may seem. All the spiritual traditions teach us to love our neighbors as ourselves and to do unto others as we would have them do unto us. We naturally want the best things for ourselves. In each situation, we can simply put ourselves in the other's shoes and assess how we would like to receive what we are offering. If we could make these shifts in perspective more often, seeing circumstances from the other's point of view, we would gain a very useful barometer for our actions. But normally we tend to look for what we want and manipulate our surroundings to fulfill our desires.

How beautiful it is when a man and woman come together

in genuine love! They can create an amazing miracle. Unfortunately, as we have seen, the majority of people on this planet do not know how to experience real heart-to-heart love. Indeed, very few people on the planet even know how to have sex, despite the fact that they are constantly exposed to sexual stimulation in everyday life. If they really knew how, why would they have to have sex with so many people? When we have a deep sexual connection with another person, we are satisfied and do not seek the excitement and novelty of someone else. But because people do not know how to relate genuinely to others, they feel empty and attempt to acquire what they lack through a series of superficial encounters.

Question: Is it valid to seek public office or a high position in a corporation or a spiritual organization? Or is it subtle sex?

Answer: It depends upon our motivation. If we are acting in order to gratify our senses and reinforce our egos, it is subtle sex. But if we are expressing our love for God and for humanity, it is service. Material aspects of life, such as fame, financial success, or sexual expression, are not bad. It is what we do with each of these that matters. Someone can be more attached to a little mat and water pot than others are to their palaces or mansions. The consciousness involved is what is important. There is nothing wrong with a profession that pursues popularity or brings distinction; the value of these factors depends on how we use them. If we forget God and feel that we are special, deserving of even more popularity and distinction, then we are on the wrong track. But if we can dedicate our success to the Lord's service, then we have more leverage and greater opportunities to help.

Question: From what you have said, I understand that much of the corruption in today's leaders, beyond sexual misconduct, can be attributed to the influence of subtle sex. Is that correct?

Answer: Yes. For example, sometimes men and women of the cloth engage in illegal or unethical behavior for their own selfish ends. In one African country I visit, certain criminals have aligned themselves with ministers, mystics, and sorcerers in order to gain a shield of protection that prevents them from being arrested or killed as they commit their crimes. After they successfully complete their criminal activity, they pay a fee to the one who assisted them.

Several years ago in Africa, predictions were made that the world was coming to an end. Religious leaders collected a lot of money warning their congregations that the end of the world was near. They instructed their followers to repent and turn over their assets to the church to compensate for their sins because, after all, the money would not be needed. Three or four days before the supposed end of the world, some of the major churches participating in that deception closed their doors and moved out of the country.

At the time, I appeared on so many television programs in Africa to discuss this topic that it became ridiculous. Many people did not want to face the end of the world in a sober state and got intoxicated. Others sold their houses to get money, as if they could take that with them. Others withdrew their money from banks and started frequenting prostitutes, attempting to enjoy as much as possible before death. It is obvious that the corruption of religious leaders caused untold chaos for those whom they were supposed to guide and enlighten. Such leaders mainly focus on their own gain, normally exploiting and cheating others in the process. They are controlled by lust and greed rather than love and selflessness.

Chapter 2

What Is Love?

All of us want to be loved with unconditional, eternal love—a love that sees beyond beauty, intelligence, or any other superficial quality. We want to be loved simply because we *are*. At the same time, we all have a natural, innate tendency to share our love with others. This preoccupation with love arises because in reality we are eternal, loving beings whose souls are filled with knowledge and bliss. In this physical embodiment we are temporarily covered by material energy, but our nature is inherently divine, and we are always seeking the blissful love of the spiritual kingdom where our real fulfillment lies.

But something always seems to go wrong. Despite our constant search, we usually experience disappointment, finding that our experience of love is temporary. Although we may have tried and failed in a variety of relationships, we persist in believing that the right person is out there somewhere. For some mysterious reason, we just never seem to be in the right place at the right time.

The World Lacks Love

Countless people in the world today have never felt truly loved. They have no idea what love really is, despite their deep longing for it. In fact, in everyday relationships, the term "love" has developed too vague a meaning and may even indicate something quite different, such as control or need. For example, the idea of love is often reduced to a mere bodily exchange or to a process of trying to gain gratification from someone else—by force if necessary. This is not love.

The problem arises because we are looking for answers in all the wrong places. We have forgotten the spiritual dimension of life. A society without a spiritual nucleus lacks the "cosmic glue" to make everything work. Love is the "cosmic glue" that holds us together as we learn to know and relate to one another and, ultimately, to the Supreme Personality of Godhead.

Modern society seems to have forgotten this. *But deep down, even though the experience of love often eludes us, we know that love is our birthright.* It is as if someone were holding something deliciously tantalizing in front of us just beyond our reach. We want it, we know it is available, but we are not quite able to grasp it. So we substitute something else, hoping to find happiness in wealth, prestige, or power. Let us look more deeply at how this works by first examining what love is not.

Love Is Not About Getting Something

Genuine love is not concerned with personal gain, but rather with the quality of the exchange between those involved. When we think only of ourselves, trying to arrange matters to get what we want, we are not expressing love. Unconditional love is never based on trying to receive anything. Instead, it is an experience of giving and a joyful activity in which each participant strives to share more generously than the other.

This point is particularly relevant for a society that frequently equates love with sex. Sex provides one of the greatest pleasures we normally experience here, and we try to enjoy it as frequently as possible. Practically every major effort to influence our consciousness is based upon trying to entice us sexually. Unfortunately, this attempt to enslave human civilization is succeeding all too well. As we have already seen, countless advertisements try to stimulate the public's sexual desire in order to boost sales. Consequently, people focus outwardly and do not attribute value to knowing each other or themselves. In fact, because they cannot get beyond the "body game," their consciousness remains enslaved and subject to physical passions.

However, love has nothing to do with the amount of sexual pleasure we can obtain from another person. Love is not about sex. People often say, "Let us make love," when they actually mean, "Let us have sex." When we believe that sex is love, then even incest becomes acceptable, because a father who loves his daughter will feel free to approach her sexually. Indeed, all over the world, incest is increasing, and as we mentioned earlier, so many of its victims carry tremendous wounds, sometimes for life.

Love has nothing to do with exploitation. It is not a business deal or an accounting system that requires the actions of one person to be balanced by those of another. Instead, love expresses genuine concern for the well-being of others. This is difficult to understand in our "gimme" society, which assumes that people always have ulterior motives for their actions.

We often settle for security relationships, which operate like a business: "You satisfy me, and I will satisfy you." Unfortunately, as soon as a disturbance arises in our contract, we are ready to seek another relationship. Ultimately, real love has nothing to do with what somebody else says or does. It is based on us—not on the other person—and is an expression of what we are, what we have, and what we can share.

When we love someone, we want to do something for that person. If we really care for our husband, our wife, our child, or our friend, we will be excited about each opportunity to serve. And once we have rendered service, we will become even more excited, because we will be happy to know we have been able to assist. Whenever a difficulty arises, we will be eager to do something for our beloved to demonstrate our caring and commitment, without expecting anything in return.

Love Is Not a Feeling

Most of us consider love to be a feeling that ebbs and flows according to the circumstances. But genuine love is not linked to what we feel, nor does it depend on any external conditions. Real love is divine, and cannot exist separately from the source, which is God.

Love is not something we can turn on and off like a faucet. In our society, we often do not understand this. A man and a woman may make marital vows, and then change their minds in a few months or years. In such a state of consciousness, we are constantly looking for something outside of ourselves instead of tapping the wellspring of love within. Although we may occasionally be disturbed by someone's actions, true love remains firm, because it is based on something far deeper than mere sentiment. When love is sentimental, any upset may suddenly turn the object of our affections into an enemy.

Many people have difficulty establishing meaningful relationships with others. Once the initial infatuation wears off, they are disappointed to discover that their relationship was reactive rather than proactive. A proactive person has vision-centered principles and a philosophical orientation, whereas a reactive person is preoccupied with self-centered concerns such as eating, sleeping, defending, and mating. Reactive people view everything in terms of personal enjoyment. For them, love is a feeling that enhances their sense of well-being so that, whenever they are not getting what they want, they withdraw.

On the other hand, when we are genuinely loving, we are not concerned with ourselves at all. Love is a verb: we empathize, appreciate, share, help, and give. We are not trying to feel good or control the environment to enhance our own pleasure.

Love Is Not Always Pleasant

Since love is not defined by our pleasant feelings, pain can be an integral part of love. Although most of us would prefer to experience happiness and eliminate pain from our relationships, this attitude is based on a desire to satisfy our senses. Genuine love can indeed bring us great happiness, yet it can also cause extreme suffering.

If we examine our lives even a little, we notice that our greatest pain has almost invariably come from relationships with those we love. Perhaps we tried to give and were not fully appreciated, or perhaps we wanted to make a loving connection and somehow could not. Who cannot remember the deep hurt of being betrayed, disappointed, neglected, or abandoned? At the same time, our greatest happiness has also come from relationships with others. *It is a paradox that love, the most healing force there is, can also make us so vulnerable to pain.*

In a loving relationship, each difficulty in our lives becomes a challenge to glorify and serve the Lord. When we care about someone, the hard times are wonderful because they demonstrate the need for greater communication. Because our partner did not receive our words or actions in a loving spirit, we see a need for love. This gives us an exciting opportunity to serve and to support the well-being of the other person.

When we are in control, we feel good about everything. But as soon as events do not go as planned, we may become unwilling to accommodate our partner. Whenever we experience doubts about the relationship, we turn away. These doubts may arise because we lack strong faith or feel insecure. Often we project our fears and phobias onto our partners and onto our environment to avoid facing the fact that the problem is within our own consciousness. Then, even if somebody gives us a compliment, we may think suspiciously, "What do you mean by that?" Some people remain entrenched in a mood of negativity no matter what happens.

Our goal as spiritual warriors is to become so loving that nothing seems to bother us. In this state, we will not be affected by negativity at all. Instead, we will be grateful for negative comments as well as praise, and may even interpret harsh words in a loving way. At first, this may seem naive. But actually, such behavior reflects strong faith in the Lord and a willingness to share our faith and love with others. All of us actually have the capacity to become so fixed in our love that everything in the environment only helps us to be more loving. This is the mood of a true spiritual warrior.

Jealousy and Envy Are Not Love

However, even in spiritual circles, people often do not understand how to love one another. Despite a seeming commitment to a spiritual lifestyle, individuals may experience envy and jealousy of their peers. For example, if one person is advancing spiritually, others who are trapped in material consciousness may be unable to feel happiness for that individual. Instead, they become jealous and mean-spirited.

People who worship fame, money, and material comforts are attached to temporary aspects of life. Ultimately, they are destined to be unhappy, because everything temporary deteriorates. They are condemning themselves to loss and frustration. This pursuit of selfish pleasures is a general feature of modern Western culture. In the process of climbing our way to the top, we are conditioned to think, "I only win when you fail." In order to build ourselves up, we are eager to see someone else's demise. We may even sabotage a potential rival, believing that this is the way to become successful.

However, we should remember that whenever we feel sad, disturbed, and envious of another's success, we are unqualified for the blessings of spiritual life. In these circumstances, we must work on ourselves to dissolve our selfish motivations, so that eventually we can reach the point of being happy and enthusiastic for the accomplishments of others. We are always enhanced rather than diminished by another person's growth.

Love Is Stronger than Doubt

Love must transcend any doubts we may have about the value of spiritual life. Persistent doubts are always detrimental to spiritual advancement, making us vulnerable to materialistic illusions and weakening our alignment with spiritual guidance and protection. This does not mean that we should be blind followers who accept spiritual teachings without question. Doubts naturally arise as we progress along the spiritual path. But to avoid the dangers inherent in prolonged, lingering doubts, we should address each question immediately as it arises. Our sincere inquiries can put doubts to rest without leaving an opening for negative influences to lead us astray.

Spiritual life requires great intensity, strong faith, and firm conviction. Unresolved doubts make the body and the mind revert to old familiar patterns, behaving just like drug addicts who return to the familiar solace of drugs whenever life becomes difficult. If our faith and strength have vanished, we naturally resort to our previous coping mechanisms to find some comfort.

Indeed, most of us are addicts. We are powerfully addicted to the senses and to our lower nature, which have been our steady companions for a long time. As we develop spiritually, we must be careful to not become unbalanced, or we may revert to old patterns. That is why we must resolve our doubts as quickly and honestly as possible.

The Source of Love

Now that we have seen what love is not, let us look more closely at what love is, and where it comes from. The origin of love can only be found in a place far beyond this material world. In fact, deep love cannot exist independently from the Supreme Lord, because He is the source and storehouse of everything. *Those who lay claim to love without a connection to the Godhead may think they have valuable diamonds but are actually in possession of only cut glass.* Because they lack the essential spiritual connection, in reality they have nothing. Genuinely spiritual people, on the other hand, are automatically loving, because they are conduits for God's own energy. As they radiate divine love, they naturally share it and help others to connect with it.

Our longing for eternal love is a sign that we are out of our natural state. This temporary earthly condition does not fulfill us, because physical bodies and material interactions always come to an end. We want to be loved eternally because we are imperishable, spiritual beings for whom love is an expression of the soul.

Ultimately, all major spiritual traditions confirm that we are loving entities who are out of place in the material world. They teach that we have a chance to experience far more love than we normally encounter in our daily lives. As we become more loving and make efforts to serve others, we gradually enter into the realm of divine love. When we offer such genuine love to others, we receive much more in return. Once we develop a deep spiritual connection, we begin to experience the greater pleasures that we had previously anticipated but did not find in material life. We discover a love that is endless, unlimited by time and circumstances, and completely fulfilling.

Unconditional Love Is Spiritual

Unconditional love, then, is beyond material concerns. It exists in a realm that transcends the mind and the body, and is related to the nature of the soul. Its natural expression is free from limitations of the body such as birth, disease, old age, and death. To experience such love, we must set aside our personal desires for sense gratification and give up taking action just to elicit a predetermined response.

Unconditional love must be just that: without conditions, unmotivated, and uninterrupted. Such love is beyond any effort to be good, upright, ethical, or moral. Many "good" people only do the right thing to gain recognition and approval. In contrast, an action based on unconditional love is one we perform even if others blame us for it. For example, a mother may know that her child does not want to stop playing to eat dinner. But, undeterred by the child's anger, she calls him into the house anyway, because she knows he needs nourishment.

The elements that make up the physical world are all part of God's separated, or external energies, and not directly related to the deeper aspects of the Divine. Pure, unmotivated love, on the other hand, is transcendental to anything material and can ultimately connect us with the Lord's potent internal energies.

In Sanskrit, we speak of *sac-cid-ananda-vigraha*, meaning that the soul is eternally absorbed in the ecstasy of love, permeated with full knowledge, and steeped in bliss. Deep love cannot exist without knowledge and appreciation. In the absence of these qualities, love becomes abstract and general. We cannot deeply love someone whom we do not know, even if we have a generally "nice" feeling about that individual. The most we can express is a sense of vague admiration.

The more we know about those we love, the more our love can be deep and substantive. Genuine love is based on an awareness of particular attributes and qualities. When we know the beloved well, we gain a profound appreciation of that person and understand how to serve most effectively. On the other hand, if we do not know much about someone, our unfamiliarity can produce difficulties because we lack the proper understanding to develop effective communication and action. In the same way, we cannot love God without a great appreciation for who the Lord is, what the Lord does, and what the Lord desires from us.

A Gathering of Sages

With all the Hollywood depictions of sentimental love so prevalent in our mechanized society, many of us have difficulty understanding the true meaning of spiritual love. We have little opportunity to go beyond a bodily relationship or to view others as anything but extensions of ourselves. These approaches to love are so pervasive that they even affect our attitude toward God. We have a tendency to think of the Lord as someone who can fulfill our personal desires, and so we have no interest in serving Him selflessly in an unmotivated, unconditional way.

The *Srimad-Bhagavatam*, an ancient and extremely sacred Vedic scripture, describes an assembly of *yogis* and great mystics from many different paths who assembled long ago in a forest in India known as Naimisaranya. They came together to address the question: "What is the highest human activity?" These *yogis* were eager to discover the most expedient processes for attaining the highest level of spiritual development. They were prepared to stay together and ponder the question for years if necessary, until they could come to some satisfactory conclusion. Despite the fact that they came from many different traditions, they all shared the common goal of wanting to experience the greatest spiritual truths. The seekers at the assembly had a deep level of sincerity. Thus they questioned a very special pure devotee of the Lord by the name of Suta Gosvami, who was completely selfless and unmotivated. In any spiritual gathering, the sincerity of both the speakers and of the audience are extremely important.

What eventually emerged from the meeting was the understanding that spirituality is never a matter of one creed or dogma versus another. The sage did not dwell on such temporary conceptions, nor did he imply that one teaching was higher than any other. Instead, he spoke of the importance of knowledge, service, and love of God beyond any externals, explaining that love and service form the true foundations for self-realization. When we love God unconditionally, we do not pray for relief from anxiety, distress, or frustration. Such prayers are not indicative of high-level devotion. Instead, we need to learn how to share our love by offering unmotivated, uninterrupted service.

Love Is Unmotivated Service

Love is far more than sweet-sounding words; love only becomes real through our behavior. We express our love by what we do. If someone professes love for another but is unwilling to serve that person, the love is not deep. It is theoretical and not genuine. If we do not demonstrate our love by dynamic activity, something is wrong. The deeper the love, the more we will express it by selfless service to the object of our love.

This understanding of love as service is fundamental to all the major world religions. Although these religions differ superficially in many respects, they are united around one central point: true religion means service to God. Whatever we call ourselves—Christian, Jew, Muslim, Buddhist, or Hindu—is not particularly significant, nor are the rituals we perform. Behind all the exterior practices is the fact that each religious path has come into being to provide us with specific ways to love and serve God.

Although love transcends seeing, hearing, and feeling, all of these elements may be incorporated into selfless service. When our love is unconditional, we do not seek a particular experience for our own benefit, as we would if we engaged in self-interested behavior to gratify our senses. Selfish actions do not allow us to develop a deeper connection with God, but are based on "my wants," "my desires," and "my body." They are not genuinely focused on the other or on rendering service to the beloved.

The more we give and share what we have, the more we put the Lord first, inconveniencing ourselves for His service. If we have little, we give a piece of bread or a glass of water. If we only have a banana, then that is what we offer. If we have anything at all to eat, then the other person should be able to eat also.

When we love someone, we want to offer care; we are eager to express what we feel inside by doing something for the object of our love. A man who loves his wife and children does not just say so; he spends time with them and cares for their needs. A woman may claim to love her husband and child, but if she does not feed her child or assist her husband, then we may rightfully doubt her sincerity.

Sometimes we may say loving words despite feelings to the contrary, in order to gain approval or the reassurance that we ourselves are loved. This behavior does not reflect either love or service. We should not speak untruthfully just to be rewarded. If our love is genuine, we will freely and wholeheartedly share ourselves with the beloved without wondering, "What's in it for me?"

If love had something to do with expecting a particular response, what would happen if we did not get the one we wanted? When we equate love with sense gratification, we risk becoming angry, morose, or disappointed whenever we are not satisfied. Yet most of us attach conditions to our love, because foremost in our minds is our own comfort. But unconditional love goes far beyond our personal satisfaction, even to the point of exposing us to great inconvenience on behalf of the beloved.

Service is natural. We are always serving someone or something, and those who love one another understandably want to express their love through service. That is why we have the Golden Rule: "Do unto others as you would have them do unto you." When we see ourselves as servants of the beloved, we seek to please the other as a spontaneous expression of our love. We are indifferent to praise or blame. But unfortunately, although we may try to serve enthusiastically, our motivation is often impure; we want to be recognized and appreciated. We must learn to serve willingly even in the absence of any reciprocation or acknowledgment.

We should remember that the way we treat others is actually the way we are treating ourselves, because everything eventually comes back to us. Why do some people always have so much help and care? Because they give it, and therefore it returns to them in kind. Why is it that no one trusts those who do not trust others? Because that distrustful energy is coming full circle back to them. We have to be careful of what we do and how we think, because our thoughts and actions set forces in motion to bring the results back to us.

We can test ourselves by doing a favor anonymously for someone we really care about. Generally, when we offer a gift, we send a card identifying ourselves as the giver and implying that we expect some measure of recognition for our generosity. Obviously, this is not selfless, unconditional behavior, because it is based on self-glorification. We can only pass the test of selfless, unmotivated service when we help someone without seeking praise, happy simply in the knowledge that we have taken the right action.

Becoming Transcendental

When we genuinely serve another person with unconditional love, we are surrendering to the will of God. We are setting our personal interests aside and doing the necessary, no matter what the cost. Because of our love, we do not react even when someone is critical or angry. We just find a more tactful way to accomplish our service. We go on being humble, which means being concerned about others and making even better arrangements for them than we would for ourselves, because we love them even more than ourselves. That is genuine unconditional love.

Such steadfast behavior means that we are becoming transcendental instead of remaining merely sentimental. We are sentimental when we are attached to feeling good, to maintaining peace at all costs, or to tolerating the misdeeds of others in order to avoid their displeasure. This is a form of sense enjoyment that is a hindrance in spiritual life. As we have seen, real love is not based on wanting to feel good, mentally, psychologically, or physically. The focus of such a superficial approach is egocentric, because we are just using a relationship, even with God, to get what we want.

We become transcendental when we rise above the material state of affairs and the platform of everyday mediocrity. We elevate ourselves by keeping our focus clear, persevering in our spiritual practices, and passing our daily tests. We do not allow obstacles, such as our own senses or those of other people, to stand in the way.

Love does not always mean that we maintain contact with another person, or that we are gentle and kind. Sometimes we must go away or speak harsh words. But such actions are soft to the heart, because the motivation is selfless. If we are capable of real love, we do not stop loving others even if we decide to be abrupt or stop associating with them. Despite appearances, our first priority should always be their highest good.

As spiritual warriors, we should always seek to raise the energy level around us. When we practice upgrading our surroundings, we progress quickly because we are radiating divinity and love wherever we go. According to the law of *karma*, whatever we give to others we will receive back in kind. Therefore, the more love we give, the more we will experience.

This brings us to the subject of empowerment. Although we may want to help others, we may not believe that we have sufficient love to give. In such situations, the Lord dwelling in our hearts can respond to our call, empowering us to serve beyond our normal capacities. Indeed, highly spiritual people do not rely solely upon their own intelligence or their normal understanding. Their deep, genuine commitment brings unlimited love, knowledge, and realization beyond their own personal limitations. That is why, when we become receptive to the Lord's help, miracles start happening.

Daily Life Is a Training Ground

The sages and *yogis* at the gathering described in the

Srimad-Bhagavatam understood, by the mercy of Suta Gosvami, that love was based on unmotivated service to God. They realized that genuine spirituality meant becoming servants of everyone. The same is true for us. In everyday life, our relationships with one another are practice for the divine relationships we will eventually experience. The quality of our interactions indicates how well we are preparing ourselves for association with the Supreme Lord. That is why association with others who are serious about spiritual life is so important. Through these experiences, we are learning to love and serve the Supreme.

The highest level of the spiritual world is a realm of eternal spiritual romance and of selfless, loving exchanges. To enter the realm of pure love, we must begin here and now in the material world to become pure, unmotivated servants. Any egocentric motivation disqualifies us, because to experience divine love we must feel joy in denying our own appetites for the pleasure of the loved one. We do not lose our own identity in the process. On the contrary, our true identity expands as we render service, and each expression of selflessness intensifies our capacity to experience ever more vast dimensions of love. When we are motivated by genuine love to act so selflessly, even more love is available to us.

Questions and Answers

Question: You mentioned that all world religions are essentially the same. Does that mean the differences don't matter?

Answer: Of course, important differences exist, based on how evolved a system is. However, sectarianism is very dangerous.

Sectarian people are implying that God only gives His love through their particular group. Are we only eligible for God's love if we are Episcopalian, Sufi, Baha'i, Hindu, or a member of some other religious system? There are many ministers, teachers and laypersons that would answer in the affirmative, believing that their teaching is the only valid one. This means that they believe God's love to be so limited that He can express it in only one way. But we cannot serve the one God in such a fragmented, sectarian way.

An analogy may help illustrate the reason for the existence of so many different religions. As parents trying to help our children, we may give them an instruction in one particular form. If they do not understand, or if they do not apply our advice properly, we may give them the instruction again in a slightly different form, because we care about them and want them to succeed. God acts in a similar fashion. He gives us the same instructions in a wide variety of ways, to ensure that we will learn to do the right thing.

If we humans can have many sons and daughters, then why should God, the supreme progenitor, have only one son? That does not make sense. In addition to Jesus, are not Muhammad and Buddha—as well as many others—also children of God? Actually, are we not all sons and daughters of the Lord? It is just that we are sons and daughters who have wandered off the path, whereas Jesus and other sons or daughters of God did not deviate at all. They tried to help those family members who went astray to come back into the fold.

All bona fide spiritual emissaries teach the Lord's message according to their commission, meaning that each one has a special assignment to fulfill. They are helping to prepare souls to serve in various areas of God's kingdom. If sectarianism were so important, millions of souls would be arguing and fighting once they arrived in the Lord's abode, saying, "Hold on a minute! Where's the place for the Seventh Day Adventists? I don't have time for anybody else!" Or, "Where are the Sunni Muslims? They are the true children of God." Everyone would be aligned in opposing camps, ready to engage in battle. In such circumstances, when would anyone ever have a chance to glorify and serve the Lord?

If Jesus appeared among us at this time in history, he might be crucified even more quickly than before. He would certainly have a lot of moneychangers to chase out of our contemporary temples all over the planet. It might not take long for Christians of various denominations to form an alliance to silence such a disturbing personality. If the Prophet Muhammad returned today, he would simply weep at the violence in the world that demonstrates profound ignorance and misunderstanding of his teachings. In the Vedic tradition, if any of the great sages and *swamis* returned to see how we were doing, they would be deeply discouraged.

Spiritual life is not about what label we give others and ourselves, how we pray, or where we worship. Instead, it is about how genuine we are. Ultimately, it does not matter what vehicle we ride in. One person may like a Chevrolet; another may prefer a Mitsubishi or a Ford; and someone else may only feel comfortable in a Jaguar. The choice is up to us. The essential point is to get to our destination through a bona fide connection.

If we have a problem aligning with someone's consciousness because of superficial differences, then we are not really interested in consciousness at all. And if we are not interested in consciousness, we are at an elementary level of evolution. Our collective state of consciousness is the crucial factor that will make the difference on this planet. The purpose of life has never been related to one's religion. Instead, it has always been concerned with one's level of spiritual development. The true struggle on this planet today is between those in a low, negative state of consciousness and those at a higher level.

Question: You talk about the material world and the spiritual world. What is the relationship between the two?

Answer: We can learn a great deal about the spiritual realm by examining the material world, which is a reflection of the genuine Kingdom of God, even though this reflection is a perverted one. Most of us, at one time or another, have experienced uplifting associations with other people. Because these encounters were so wonderful, our thoughts became preoccupied with the person we were with, and we yearned to be in that individual's company again. Sometimes our daydreams were so blissful that they carried us through many dull, boring, or painful periods in our lives.

In a similar way, when we encounter difficulties in material life, we can remind ourselves that our original constitutional position is in the spiritual kingdom—an abode of pure, unending love and devotion. Our awareness of the joys of spiritual realization can help us move through the temptations and difficulties that we have to experience at this present time.

Even a single day, a single week, or a single year can seem endless when things are not going well. But from the vantage point of eternity, this lifetime is just a small distraction, a temporary blip. Once we are back in the spiritual kingdom, the countless years that we passed in lower realms of existence will merely seem like flickering moments of a nightmare.

So if we are suffering, experiencing difficulties far greater than we can bear, we can make eternal life our point of reference and almost laugh at our troubles. We can remind ourselves that at some point in our evolution we will have a chance to become pure, so that all our present problems will vanish just as nightmares eventually do. It is as if we were in the spiritual world now, but dozed off for a while. The experience of "nodding off" is what we are now undergoing in this material world, which seems filled with never-ending complications, miseries, and challenges.

We can change our experience by turning away from relative material concerns and understanding more about transcendental love, which we can only appreciate as we deepen our knowledge of the soul. As we elevate our consciousness and become more transcendental, then all our current difficulties in the material world will fade into insignificance.

Question: To what extent do our attitudes toward money influence our attitudes toward love?

Answer: That is a nice question, because it has a lot to do with contemporary society. People who are unwilling to give financially probably will not give in other ways, either. Finances are just one aspect of a deeper problem. Those who refuse to share their money with their mates are most likely selfish in other aspects of their relationship. In a marriage, spouses should be generous with each other, considering everything as belonging to God, and therefore to their partners as well.

We have all heard the saying, "Money is the honey." But actually, apart from what it symbolizes, money itself has little to do with love, although it can be a source of frustration that interferes with one's expression of love. Divorce often occurs because of financial problems, and worries about money can cause tension in a family to the point that people cannot share their higher love. A husband and wife can focus so much on the mortgage, the insurance, or the car that they forget about love and service. Communication disintegrates because each person is distracted, thinking, "Two more days, then I've got to make the car payment."

A relationship is not deep if a couple can only function when everything is going well. The real tests come as difficulties arise, when both parties have the greatest need to receive love and to feel loved. Some people will allow problems to drive them further apart. But those who are truly loving will bond together even more, trying to be more selfless and denying themselves for each other. A woman might choose to not get a new dress so that her husband can get a new pair of pants. A father might choose to not get a car because he wants his child to go to a special school. Such sacrifices, which are expressions of love, help foster strong, close relationships.

Chapter 3

What Is Lust?

The ancient *Bhagavad-gita* takes the form of a long conversation between the Lord and the warrior Arjuna. As Arjuna inquires about the spiritual truths of existence, the Lord offers important insights into the nature of lust. Arjuna, a great disciple of the Lord, is rebelling against his responsibility to fight a major battle because many of the enemies are his family members, mentors, and friends. At the last minute, poised for battle, Arjuna refuses to fight. Paralyzed by grief and anguish, he asks the Lord, who is playing the role of his charioteer, to explain what he should do. In one particular verse (*Bhagavad-gita* 3.36), Arjuna inquires:

arjuna uvaca
atha kena prayukto 'yam
papam carati purusah
anicchann api varsneya
balad iva niyojitah

> *By what is one impelled to sinful acts, even unwillingly, as if engaged by force?*

Arjuna wants to know what causes human beings to act in harmful ways despite their good intentions.

Most people wonder what sometimes causes us to act against our better judgment? Haven't we all said to ourselves, "Why did I do that? Why did I hurt that person? Why did I fly off the handle?" We want to be ethical and moral, and we want to live an exemplary life, no longer taking drugs, drinking, insulting our spouse, being a chauvinist, or abusing others. But despite the fact that we promise ourselves never to engage in such behavior again, we still persist in the same undesirable patterns. Arjuna wants to know what provokes such contrariness.

In the next verse of the *Bhagavad-gita*, the Lord gives the answer, explaining to Arjuna that "lust only" is the cause of our sinful behavior. Originally, we come into contact with lust just by being born into this world, a place where our eternal love of God turns into lust simply by its encounter with material energy. That is to say, our inherent, natural love for God becomes lust just as milk turns into curd when it comes in contact with lemon juice. Lust is actually an egocentric misdirection of the love that is our birthright—a love inherent in all creation. Because we are part and parcel of a loving God, in our natural state we share in that love. Here in the material world, though, we are not in our natural state, and the self-centered energy of lust has caused us to forget our birthright.

Suffering in the Material World

Suffering is an inherent aspect of being born into the material world. In the Kingdom of God, the problems of old age, disease, and death do not exist. How can there be imbalance or disorder in the Kingdom of God? Our miseries are consequences of our physical embodiment, not of our spiritual nature.

Imagine that someone said to you, "I want to send you to an interesting place. It's one where people constantly kill each other, races fight one another, tribes struggle against each other, and men and women compete against one another. It's a place that becomes so hot you can have a sunstroke and die, or so cold you can freeze to death. You might be harassed by insects, rats, snakes, and spiders, and one species is constantly devouring another just to eat." This is the nature of our present environment; it is very hellish. An intelligent person who has a choice would not want to come to such a terrible place.

Sometimes we can see a bird in our own back yard swoop down and grab an insect for dinner. Just imagine how it would feel to be that insect. One afternoon in Lagos, Nigeria, I was sitting quietly on a porch, when my eyes fell upon some ants and a beetle. As I watched, the beetle quickly ate the ants, and immediately a grasshopper appeared and ate the beetle. Then all of a sudden a bird flew down and ate the grasshopper. This little drama occurred in a matter of minutes, and it gave me an even greater realization of how one species constantly abuses another in a universal struggle for survival.

The Material Universe Is Not Our Home

This earthly realm, so filled with suffering, cannot bring us happiness. That is why the Bible tells us to not love this world or the things of this world. All bona fide prophets, including Jesus, Muhammad, Buddha, and many other great teachers, deliver the same threefold message. Using different terminologies, they teach us to love God with all our hearts, to love our neighbors as ourselves, and to seek the Kingdom of God, which is our true home.

Jesus said, "Our Father, who art in heaven." By saying, "Our Father," Jesus has made it clear that each of us has connections in the spiritual world just as he does. We all have a common origin and home. But as long as we are covered by lust, we forget this truth and live like criminals sentenced to a long prison term, reincarnating over and over again as we search for peace and happiness in all the wrong places.

Since in our original state we are all pure servants of God, whatever else we have become is temporary, part of the contamination that we have imposed upon ourselves lifetime after lifetime. Once we identify with the material world, we are subject to its problems and errors. We cannot have sufficient love for God if we become too attached to the things of this world, because we cannot serve God and mammon simultaneously. If our minds are filled with lustful thoughts of material pleasures, then there is little room for spirituality to enter our consciousness. That is why the saints have told us throughout millennia to simplify our lives with simple living and high thinking. We must always engage in purifying our consciousness; otherwise we will not have room for higher realizations.

We Are Accountable

The choice of God or mammon is always up to us. Although we may blame external forces for our addictive, manipulative, or selfish activities, we cannot escape our own ultimate responsibility. Even in extreme cases where people actually become possessed, hear voices, or fall into a trance as the body moves uncontrollably, these apparent victims of demonic energies are accountable for their situation. Although they may explain, truthfully, that their behavior was beyond their control, they forget that they did make choices that led to this condition in the first place. Negative forces are attracted wherever there is a receptive lower consciousness.

Even in less dramatic situations we make excuses, saying that "something came over" us, that we were subjected to demonic influences, or that we fell under the spell of *maya*— another name for illusion. But despite appearances, we are always responsible for our actions. Would we try to rationalize our behavior in a court of law by explaining, "Judge, it wasn't my fault. The devil made me do it?" Of course not. The judge never says, "Well, that's all right. I'll just put the devil in jail instead of you."

What causes one person to act immorally while another does not? Both individuals may face the same temptations, yet one succumbs while the other resists, or one gives in occasionally while the other yields on a regular basis. The difference can be found in each person's level of commitment to spiritual life, which increases the level of resistance to the negative influences.

If we open ourselves to the Lord, we are acting spiritually. When we elevate our consciousness, our love and spirituality act as a block to keep negativity away. But if we open the door to sin, then we become possessed by a sinful consciousness. Sin can never be considered greater than righteousness. If we say that the "devil" made us behave badly, we are implying that the devil is more powerful than God. This is never true, and only seems to be true at times because of the impure state of our consciousness.

The Gradual Path of Degradation

How did we become so impure? As the Lord explains in the *Bhagavad-gita* 3.37:

> *kama esa krodha esa*
> *rajo-guna-samudbhavah*
> *mahasano maha-papma*
> *viddhy enam iha vairinam*

> *It is lust only, Arjuna, which is born of contact with the material modes of passion and later transformed into wrath, and which is the all-devouring sinful enemy of this world.*

Because lust causes us to lose our sanity, we often behave in ways beneath our original nature, and then our lust becomes compounded with anger. Let us see how this works.

If we do not give and receive love in a natural way that is in alignment with our spiritual birthright, our love turns into lust, which forces us to act in ways that we would not normally accept. Then, because we feel forced, we become depressed, demoralized, unfulfilled, and, consequently, angry. Deep down,

What Is Lust?   79

we know that lust can never fulfill us, but we become addicted. It is a vicious cycle: the more we give in to lust, the more we grow accustomed to it and then the demands of lust increase.

It is similar to taking a drug. At first we may yield to temptation just to see what will happen. We may even have to force ourselves to tolerate such a damaging substance, but after we become habituated, we begin to enjoy it. Eventually, we find that we need more of the drug to get the same level of stimulation as before. Lust is like that. The more we succumb to it, the more it takes control, until finally we no longer engage in sinful actions for the pleasure, but just to avoid the pain.

For example, someone who smokes a cigarette for the first time may feel sick, and a person taking a first drink often does not like the taste. Do you remember trying these substances? When you took your first cigarette, you probably huffed, puffed, coughed, choked, or lost your breath. Most likely your first drink tasted terrible or made you feel nauseated. However, if you kept smoking or drinking, you may have started liking the taste and enjoying the side effects. We become quickly conditioned to these habits because they are socially acceptable, even "cool," and because we experience a state of altered consciousness that makes us feel more relaxed than usual. Eventually our lust takes control of us to the point that we become addicted to the experience and cannot easily give these substances up.

We do not realize that lust has seduced us into a dependency that will ultimately destroy our health and well-being. In the beginning, we may simply be struggling to cope with life or to create a sense of belonging. We take a drink or ingest a drug in order to numb ourselves, to feel better, or to gain acceptance in a group. But the power of lust is so great that eventually we lose control and our addiction takes over. Indeed, lust has destroyed many people who thought they "had it together," causing them to lose their businesses, their political positions, their families, their sanity, and even their lives.

People naturally want access to higher levels of consciousness and intense experiences beyond the normal or the mundane. In contemporary society where genuine love is a rarity, is it any wonder that so many of us seek artificial stimulation to fill the void? Genuine love can be intoxicating. A person in love is single-minded, determined, and sometimes a bit giddy. For example, immediately after talking to our beloved on the phone, we may find ourselves skipping and dancing, and if someone we care about does us a favor or pays us a compliment, our spirits are high. But when love is absent, we may seek intoxication by other means, such as alcohol, drugs, or sex.

Other Ways Lust Tricks Us

It is easy to become addicted to substances, such as cigarettes or alcohol, even if they are initially unpleasant. In other circumstances, sinful activity may appear extremely attractive right from the outset, and we may succumb without thinking of the consequences. For example, if we see a beautiful diamond ring that we want to own but cannot afford, our desire may become so strong that we forget about anything else. We think only, "Wouldn't it be nice to have that ring? How wonderful it will look on my finger! How envious people will be!"

The mind has convinced us that owning the ring will bring great pleasure, and so we steal it without thinking of the consequences. However, circumstances change quickly. Once we have left the store with the ring, feeling entranced by our new possession, a police car suddenly pulls up beside us on the street. The jeweler has sounded the alarm, and we are unceremoniously arrested and thrown in jail. As we sit in our cell, we have plenty of time to wonder, "Mind, how did you get me into this mess?" We are left in an even more painful situation than when we started.

Although we felt unhappy without the ring, we bring ourselves far more misery by stealing it and suffering the subsequent consequences. The end result is similar to the one encountered by alcoholics. A person who becomes accustomed to the taste of alcohol may drink to enjoy an altered state of consciousness and to forget life's troubles. Although the experience is initially pleasurable, eventually it becomes a painful addiction. The alcoholic drinks to maintain a precarious sense of balance, to avoid feeling sick, to numb the pain, or to stop the shaking. Whether we steal, drink, or indulge in other forms of sense gratification, the ultimate outcome is often far worse than the original condition we were trying to escape.

This is how lust keeps us trapped. Once we give in, the mind tricks us again and again. It knows our weaknesses and whispers to us seductively, "Here is your chance…You know you want to…Go for it!" If our mind does not have access to our intelligence—the faculty of discernment—we will repeatedly fall prey to these temptations. Some people attempt to stop drinking for years, resolving every morning to not take another drink. Yet before the day is over, they have reverted to their old habits. Others have spent most of their lives in jail, because every time they are released, their passion and lust cause them to commit crimes again despite all resolutions to the contrary.

Triumphing Over Lust

We must watch ourselves carefully if we are to escape the clutches of lust. To halt the downward progression of our consciousness, we must not allow our lust to degrade into anger and self-perpetuating illusion, from which it is extremely difficult to escape. People who have conquered lust can accomplish amazing feats, because their self-control connects them with the energy of love. They become empowered spiritual warriors who are extremely difficult to defeat. On the other hand, those under the influence of lust are easily manipulated. For example, a boxer may deliberately try to make his opponent angry in order to cause him to lose control and lunge, with no thought for the consequences. This is just what the fighter wants: to have his opponent open and undefended, ready for defeat.

Material energy, in the guise of the devil or *maya*, likes to make people lose control so they become easy prey. Consequently, we must monitor ourselves, being careful to not allow lust to make us lose mastery over any situation. Like the boxer just mentioned, a warrior who loses control becomes a casualty. A soldier who gets angry on the battlefield may suddenly leap out of his foxhole and run toward the enemy, shouting, "I'm going to kill all of them!" Of course, he is the one who will soon be dead.

To avoid falling into these traps, and to live fully as human beings, we must learn to control our lust by regulating the senses. Lust hides out in the senses, looking for a chance to take advantage of us. It can cause us to lose every ounce of equilibrium and stability we have and can drive us to commit the most heinous actions, even murder or suicide. As we have seen, the more we give in to lust, the more difficult it is the next time to resist, and the more enslaved and conditioned we become—to the point that we may spend the rest of our lives in its clutches.

The senses function in an interesting way. They can be compared to horses pulling a chariot, each one straining in a different direction to make the chariot move. Any one horse pulling too strongly can cause disaster. The senses are so powerful that any unregulated or improperly controlled situation can cause an individual to commit sinful actions.

What holds our senses—the horses—in check? It is the mind, governed by the intelligence when it is in contact with the soul. The intelligence, as just mentioned, is our faculty of discernment. Human beings function according to an ascending hierarchy in the following order: the senses, the mind, the intelligence, and finally the soul. Like a skillful enemy, lust hides out in the senses, the mind, and the intelligence, waiting for an opportunity to dominate us and cover our awareness of the soul.

The mind serves as an intermediary between the intelligence and the senses, and accepts or rejects stimulation from the environment according to the quality, caliber, and strength of our intelligence. In response to the environment, the senses—the eyes, nose, ears, mouth, and genitals—send messages to the mind, demanding that the mind arrange for their gratification. The mind is constantly engaged in accepting one demand and rejecting another—accepting, rejecting, accepting, rejecting. A mind that is not sufficiently strong will give in to the senses repeatedly. A strong mind will refuse to become a slave to the senses.

We often have difficulty keeping the mind under control, even when we manage to refrain from speaking inappropriately or stop ourselves from taking an unwise action. *Everything in our lives is based on quality of mind:* who we are now, who we were before, who we are going to be, and to what degree we are bound or liberated. The mind either interferes with self-realization or serves the soul. *It can be our greatest enemy or our greatest friend.* Nothing is more devastating than a mind out of control, because the mind knows all of our secrets. An enemy who is this close to us can be very destructive! But a mind under control becomes our greatest friend for the same reason: it knows us intimately. A close friend is a source of great comfort and support. The mind's choice of direction is up to each of us.

How do we develop a strong mind? We do so by backing up the mind with the intelligence, which acts as the moral factor. The senses may have a particular desire and give the mind orders to arrange to have that desire fulfilled. However, the intelligence warns the mind, "But if you do this, these are the consequences." When the intelligence is connected with transcendental knowledge, it has sufficient power to harness the wild mind. In such circumstances, the mind will calm down and regulate the senses properly. But if the intelligence is weak, the mind will not listen. Instead, it will fall prey to the dictates of the senses.

When we have gained sufficient mastery of the senses by developing a strong mind and intelligence, we can elevate our consciousness. On the other hand, if we lack mastery, we will find ourselves on a downward slope toward animal-like behavior. Animals are extremely concerned with territorial rights and attacking others to protect their sovereignty. Humans in a low state of consciousness act in the same way. We attain a significant point in our evolution when we can break out of these animalistic shackles. We do so by developing our intelligence and tempering it with humility. Humility is a powerful weapon, because it opens us up to greater love, concern, and compassion so that we naturally become more interested in the welfare of others. Without humility, we fall prey to an inflated idea of our own importance and seek unabashedly to fulfill our egocentric desires.

Regulation of our senses steadies us in such a way that we can deal calmly with any situation without losing our higher consciousness. Each challenge simply becomes an opportunity to use the mastery we have developed. If we have such mastery, God will always give us an opportunity to practice it. If we really want to love God more and more, He will give us many challenges and tests that allow us to grow. If our mastery is weak or if our motivations are mixed, we will not pass these tests and will quickly revert to our bad patterns.

Spiritual Strength Conquers the Senses

Ultimately, then, we control lust by spiritual means. The intelligence, mind, and senses must be subject to direction from the soul. As the *Bhagavad-gita* 3.43 explains, "Thus knowing oneself to be transcendental to the material senses, mind and intelligence . . . one should steady the mind by deliberate spiritual intelligence and thus—by spiritual strength—conquer this insatiable enemy known as lust."

Our physical bodies are actually prison suits not directly associated with God. In the Bible, the Book of Corinthians says that we have a terrestrial form and a celestial one. While we are in the terrestrial body, we are away from God. The body—with its senses, mind, and intelligence—makes relentless demands upon us, and our soul has to deal with this continuous onslaught. That is why the scriptures warn us to master our senses and to not identify with our immediate environment. If we do not control our senses and identify with our material surroundings instead, we will be pulled in many directions simultaneously and lose our balance. The qualities of simplicity, renunciation, and austerity, which are part of all spiritual systems, can help us detach from such temptations and overcome lust. They allow the soul, rather than our senses, to direct our actions.

The Supersoul in the Heart

Whenever the soul is in charge rather than the senses, it is because we have become receptive to the Lord's will. Indeed, the Lord never abandons us. An active, loving presence of God listens, watches, observes, and guides us from within—if we are willing to listen. In Christianity, this presence is known as the Holy Spirit, and in the Vedic tradition it is called the Supersoul. The Supersoul communicates with the individual soul within each of us whenever we make ourselves available. This is a wonderful state of affairs, because it means that God is close enough to hear us when we are lonely and to appreciate us when no one else seems to care. In fact, the Lord's presence in the heart is the only real comfort we have. External supports may disappoint us when we need them the most, but God will never fail us—although we may fail God by not taking advantage of His love and protection.

Clinging to our own personal will only causes one problem after another. Ultimately, the way to gain mastery over the senses and begin the transformation of lust into love is to surrender to the Lord, praying, "Thy will be done." In this way, we become receptive to the guidance of the Supersoul. When we practice this prayer of surrender, we become more detached from our own will and more available to God.

How do we attain a state of surrender that seems so remote from our current situation? Several steps are available to us. First of all, we must become more willing to abide by the laws of the spiritual world. We must also associate with spiritual people who can guide us and remind us of our commitments. Finally, we must not allow anything or anyone—including our own mind and intelligence—to impede our progress toward the goal of loving and serving God.

Sometimes, even our closest friends may prove to be obstacles. At other times, the obstacle may take the form of money, and on other occasions our own husband, wife, or children may stand in the way. Their resistance may become so intense that every time we engage in spiritual activities, they complain, "Why are you always reading spiritual books? Why do you always meditate? Why do you just want to pray or chant whenever we want to do something?"

Such people are really saying, "Why does it have to be God all the time? Why not me?" A husband who wants his wife to devote all her attention to him may try to push God out of the way. A wife may behave in a similar manner. But no one can compete with God, and we are all held responsible for our choices. Our environments have been arranged by the Lord as part of our tests to ascertain our behavior in each situation.

Passing the Lord's Tests

Do we put God first in all circumstances? The Lord will test us to find out. We should not think that the great spiritual leaders of history were the only ones to be tested! Just as Job, in the Bible, underwent severe trials, we all have challenges that give us the opportunity to demonstrate the level of our commitment to spiritual life. The stories about Job's difficulties are not merely about events that happened to somebody else. They are for us to study and ponder in order to be better prepared for our own trials. If we analyze and understand Job's ordeals, we can learn how to be successful despite our own difficulties. Then when challenges arise, we can smile, realizing, "Here is my chance to get more mercy from the Lord. Here is my chance to prove my dedication and to demonstrate that I'm *in* the world, but not *of* it."

Of course, we can also fail our tests by remaining attached to this world, which means that we are not yet receptive to God's will. Remember, the Lord tests us to discover whether we are willing to put Him first no matter what. That is why we should remain calm if we have no money, no food, nobody to talk to most of the time, nobody to laugh with, or nobody with whom to share our lives. This has all been arranged by the Lord, and there is a reason for the situation we are facing that is higher than we can discern. If there were no greater reason, God would be making a mistake in our circumstances. If we accept that proposition, then we must believe that God acts foolishly and cheats us sometimes. But this is not correct—we make mistakes, not God.

There is a divine order in the apparent inequality of one person's great abundance and another's unending misery. The Lord notices what we do with what He gives us. He also wants to see how we behave if He takes something away. When everything seems to be going well, we should be careful not to fall into the trap of saying selfishly, "All praises to You, Lord! You are so wonderful! Now, bring me more stuff!" If we maintain that attitude, we are apt to curse the Lord, or wonder if there really is a God at all, when He takes everything away.

The Temptation of Jesus

Remember the story in the Bible of Satan's efforts to tempt

What Is Lust? 89

Jesus? When Jesus had fasted for many days, preparing to accomplish his greatest works, Satan tried to distract him with ideas of material gain, saying words to this effect: "You're supposed to be a son of God, and you're hungry. If God loves you, certainly you can turn these rocks into food." If Jesus had been a materialist, he might have agreed and used his powers for personal sense gratification. In more recent times, communists also exploited this approach, saying to hungry people, "So, you are spiritual? Then pray to your God for bread." Then they would provide bread from the market, saying, "Here. Now where is your God? Who is your real well-wisher?"

If we give priority to material life, we can easily become distracted, because temptations will bewilder us over and over again. But Jesus was not upset by his situation in the desert, nor was he disturbed by the devil's temptations. He did not seek mystic powers, but instead offered himself unconditionally to the Lord without expectation of reward. Consequently, he was unmoved by Satan's admonitions.

Accounts of the temptations of spiritual masters can serve as examples to prepare us for our own trials and to teach us how to remain calm and steady in happiness or distress. When we can remain equipoised in all situations, we no longer need to be tested, and the Lord will place us in more pleasing circumstances. However, if we keep finding ourselves in painful circumstances, suffering from intense loneliness, for example, then we should understand that we have not resolved certain entrenched negative patterns.

Normally, we notice what we lack. We think, "Lord, I've been fasting; I've been praying; I've been crying my eyes out. When are You going to notice me? You can tell that my eyes are red, my voice is choked up, and my knees are sore. How long does it take You to give me what I want?" The thought never crosses our minds that the Lord might be giving us what we need, even though it may not be what we desire. Our lack of gratitude only prolongs our suffering. We should try to discover the Lord's mercy in all our circumstances, however difficult they may be. He is offering us an opportunity to grow.

Different Degrees of Lust

Lust touches every living being in this material world. Indeed, we can categorize various species of life according to the degrees of lust that cover their consciousness. The *Bhagavad-gita* 3.38 explains:

> *dhumenavriyate vahnir*
> *yathadarso malena ca*
> *yatholbenavrto garbhas*
> *tatha tenedam avrtam*

> *As fire is covered by smoke, as a mirror is covered by dust, or as the embryo is covered by the womb, the living entity is similarly covered by different degrees of this lust.*

A tree or any other plant is compared to an embryo covered by the womb. These particular forms of life experience almost total imprisonment. The second category, animal life, is in a position resembling a mirror covered by dust. Animals have a higher consciousness than plants, so that the lust covering them can be more easily removed, just as it is easier to remove dust from a mirror than to bring a fetus out of the womb.

The last classification refers to human beings. Sometimes a fire generates smoke so thick that we cannot see the flames. But if we fan the fire, the flames become stronger and the smoke dissipates. Human beings are not as covered over as plants and animals. If we light a match to set a small fire, a strong wind can spread the flames and burn down a house or even a great forest. Similarly, God consciousness is capable of developing in human beings to grand proportions from a tiny spark. However, if we do not stimulate that potential by "fanning the flames," the spark will not develop sufficiently to make a fire.

Continuing with this analogy, we have the choice of raising our level of consciousness by means of spiritual activities, or of allowing our spiritual spark to become extinguished. Sometimes a spark leaps out of the fire and burns itself out on the ground. In the same way, when we move too far away from the source—our natural connection with God—we are heading toward disaster.

Importance of the Human Form

Although all life forms on Earth are affected by different degrees of imprisonment in the material world, the human platform is exceptional, and human beings have an important role to play. The Bible corroborates this, saying that humans have dominion over other living beings on this Earth. The word "dominion" here does not imply a right to exploit or abuse, but it does indicate that the human condition has special meaning.

What is so unusual about a human being? According to the *Vedas*, there are 8,400,000 varieties of life forms that the soul can occupy. Among these, the human form is the primary one that can serve as an "escape vessel." This means that souls have greater potential to free themselves from the cycle of birth and death while in a human body. An animal or plant that dies moves up to the next species automatically through the spiritual evolutionary process. According to Vedic teachings, human beings are especially endowed with sufficient ability to make inquiries about self-realization and to learn how to obtain relief from suffering, disease, old age, and death.

God's Help Is Always Available

As human beings, we must make intelligent use of this precious opportunity. We can do so if we remember that the Lord is present in our hearts as the Holy Spirit or Supersoul, providing us loving guidance. When we are selfless, the Lord knows. Conversely, as we have seen, the Lord is aware of our improper behavior, too, and we will be held accountable. If we are feeling lonely, depressed, forsaken, or overburdened, we must remember that this particular kind of test is being given to us to see how we respond.

As we pass our tests, we experience greater happiness and joy. We are beginning to experience higher pleasures by connecting with the reservoir of all pleasure, the Supreme Lord. To prepare ourselves for going back home to Godhead, we must attune ourselves to the spiritual world while still in this material environment. Such attunement means that we learn to become selfless rather than selfish, compassionate rather than cruel, and free from the clutches of greed, lust, and anger.

Lust never fulfills us. We have seen how it works. *Lust turns into anger; anger turns into illusion; and illusion attracts us over and over again into the confusion of being separate from God.* We can interrupt this endless cycle only by making a firm commitment to convert the lust back into its original form of love.

Questions and Answers

Question: Lust is love, and love comes from God. So if I am feeling lusty, or acting in a lusty way, does this mean that what I really want is God?

Answer: Yes. It means that even the greatest cheaters, abusers, manipulators, alcoholics, or drug addicts really want God in their deepest inner consciousness. Their focus is just misdirected. We all want to be with our best friend in the most beautiful environment there is. We all long for perfect reciprocation, perfect love, and perfect happiness. Ultimately, we must learn that all such perfection can only be found with God.

Although we are all looking for the same thing, lust improperly directs our energies and distorts our behavior. Since lust is merely misplaced love, nothing exists in this material creation except love in various degrees of disarray. That is why we all feel a little empty: we all long to be more loved. If someone says, "I love you; I love you; I love you," we respond, "Oh, tell me again. Say it more slowly. Say it more romantically. Say it with more feeling. Oh, please, tell me I'm your greatest love. And promise that I'll always be the most important person in your life. And keep on reminding me."

We are always looking for love, because love is the only quality that is actually missing in our lives. Unfortunately, because we are covered with lust, we keep trying to find that love outside of ourselves: in drugs, alcohol, prestige, wealth, power, or countless other misguided ways. But these substitutes never make us happy. We will only be fulfilled when we discover pure, unadulterated love, which is always available if we know where to look for it.

Question: All around me I see competition and the drive to get to the top. I see it in myself, too. Now that I am listening to you, I wonder if it is foolish to engage in such behavior when we're all in such a fallen state to begin with?

Answer: Yes. Actually, from the perspective of more evolved beings in other realms, we are all handicapped and at a primitive level of evolution. Our gross material bodies are not refined, and yet in our egocentric way we are extremely proud of them. Just think about it: our physical bodies are filled with stool, urine, pus, blood, and parasites. What is there to be proud of? It is idiotic to be conceited about belonging to a certain race, or about our physique, the color of our eyes, or the length of our hair. Given that we are all in prison, why should we be proud because our prison suit is a little lighter, darker, taller, or shorter? It is still a prison suit.

Until we realize our true condition, we can never become properly spiritual. As long as we have difficulty understanding that material life is bondage, we will have to wear prison suits of different qualities until we get exhausted. Many souls do just that, moving from an Asian body to a European body to an African body to an Indian body and back again. That is why the great prophets come into this environment and try to get us out of this place.

We must experience that which we reject or condemn in order to evolve. If we demonstrate a lack of respect for the opposite sex, we must come back again as the other sex to experience that polarity more fully. The most racist people now may be reborn as members of the race they abhor. Many slave masters or people who were involved in the slave trade have had to reincarnate in black bodies to help counteract what they have done, just as many Nazis have returned as Jews and many early American settlers have come back as Native Americans.

Materially speaking, people are not all alike. Everybody is different—even twins. Each soul has an individual identity. But at the same time, as parts and parcels of God, all souls are qualitatively the same, whatever the covering—whether the body is infantile, adult, male, female, black, or white. If we are serious about spiritual development, we must focus on the soul. As long as we put the body first, we will continue to be prisoners until we become exhausted with our suffering and are ready to learn how to live like free men and women.

Being free means living as spiritual beings. Spiritual beings do not get caught up in the suffering that the rest of us must experience for our growth. Instead, they learn from it. If you do not want to grow, you might as well admit that you are comfortable in your prison. That is all right; it just has nothing to do with spiritual life.

Question: How can you or other spiritual teachers help us conquer lust?

Answer: In countless ways. Just remember that we are not interested in teaching you how to remain a slave or a prisoner. We love you too much to play the illusion game with you. We are not going to pat you on the back about how well you are enjoying your prison house. You have come to the wrong place if you want somebody to stroke you because you have beautiful blue eyes, nice Afro hair, a powerful physique, or a beautifully shaped body.

Your body is already starting to fall apart; just look in the mirror. What do you think is going to happen twenty, thirty, or forty years from now? You may have trouble walking; you may have difficulty sleeping; or you may find it hard to eat. For all the care you give your physical body, sooner or later it will deteriorate. So why should you work overtime helping to perpetuate your attachment to something temporary? It is your soul that will remain with you, and that is what connects you with God.

If you do not want to be beautiful in a spiritual way, do not bother pondering these discussions any further. Our commission—our responsibility as spiritual mentors—is to give you knowledge about how to go back to the spiritual world. If we fail to do that, we are held accountable. Therefore, if we see problems and do not address them, we are not fulfilling our mission and are instead accepting hypocrisy. When ministers, priests, prophets, or other spiritual leaders tolerate hypocrisy, they become hypocrites themselves.

We do not coerce; we apply no pressure. But we serve as constant mirrors for you to gaze into, reminding you that you are not this body, that you are spiritual beings connected with God, and that you are eternal. We are of no help if we simply reinforce your belief that you are a temporary body. No one is temporary in essence; we are eternal beings who are just carrying some temporary baggage.

If you want to make your temporary baggage a priority, then go where people encourage such a mentality. They may tell you that you are special because of your blue eyes and blond hair, or because of your African-American or Jewish heritage, or because you were born wealthy, etc. Nonsense. You are special because you are connected with God, because you are His servant. We are all children of the Lord, and everyone is part of the Lord's family.

Remember, we must put nothing before God. That is the value of associating with spiritual people, especially spiritual warriors: they can encourage each other to deepen their love, to put nothing before the Lord, and to recognize that the soul is the real person, not the body. We are all beautiful and we are all eternal.

Chapter 4

The Power of Sense Gratification

Our senses are extremely powerful. A simple story taken from the *Vedas* illustrates the persistent attraction most of us feel to the material world and its pleasures. There was once a Muslim emperor named Akbar, who was curious to know how long a person remains covered by lust. Akbar's minister, a wise old man, explained to the emperor, *"Lust is powerful for as long as you are in the material body, almost until the moment of death."* Promising an instructive example, the minister invited the emperor to go with him to a nearby hospital and to bring his beautiful daughter along. When they arrived, the minister said, "Just look at the man lying in the next room. Within the hour he will be dead. Watch him closely as we walk into the room." From the moment the three of them—Akbar, his daughter, and the minister—entered the room, the dying man could not keep his eyes off the attractive young woman. Akbar immediately understood.

Such is the power of the senses. Because they are so strong, we cannot easily defeat them or give them up. If we do not direct our energies properly, the senses will enslave us. When we are enslaved, we cannot develop our higher faculties and will not experience the ultimate transcendental pleasure that comes from loving God. We must learn to redirect our senses by making a simple change, as if we were tuning to a different radio station. The original energies still exist, but we are channeling them differently. When we offer higher pleasures to our senses, we can eventually become free of our lower desires.

Developing the Higher Taste

Spiritual life can never be only a matter of renunciation because we inherently are pleasure-seeking beings. Instead, it must become a process of energy conversion in which we reject lower, material satisfactions in favor of more spiritual pleasures. This process of substituting higher spiritual experiences for material enjoyment involves developing a higher taste. At points during this substitution process, we can become impatient, wondering when we are ever going to experience that higher taste. Of course, being habituated to our usual pursuits, we would prefer to have the higher experiences first; then we might be willing to give up the lower attachments. Often we are afraid to renounce our flickering, temporary pleasures because we believe we may be left with nothing.

Such fears mean that we are not ready to let go of our material attachments; our capacity to experience the genuine higher pleasures has not matured yet. If our approach to life continues to be one of seeking sense gratification and ego dominance, our spiritual progress will stagnate. But if we understand that life is about something far greater than material satisfaction, we will develop patience and not allow ourselves to be deterred by fears or temporary setbacks.

This analogy may help: If we expect someone to give us a thousand dollars, we can easily become attached to our expectation. We may become upset if the money does not manifest. We may lose a friendship or even take legal action as a result. On the other hand, if we are not attached to the money but focus on our friendship instead, we can remain open to the possibility that the thousand dollars may come this week or next month—or perhaps not at all. Then we are pleasantly surprised if the money does eventually appear.

Normally, we feel justified in making demands because we believe that we are the center of the universe. When we behave in this way, we are propagating the disease that brought us into this material world in the first place. This disease is our desire to be God. Although the Lord actually owns everything, we think that this world belongs to us and can be used for self-gratification. We do not understand that we are here to offer everything back to the Lord as a way of expressing our deep gratitude for what He has given us.

A Parable: The Mouse and the Sage

There is a story from the *Vedas* concerning a mouse and a sage. The sage possessed mystic powers and could fulfill the wishes of others. Of course, wishes can be dangerous, because what we ask for is often not what we really want. If someone answers our request in an unexpected way, we may become upset. We want to have everything follow our plans exactly so that we can maintain the illusion of control.

In the story, the young mouse was severely distressed because a cat constantly chased him. In desperation, he went to see the sage for help. We are all familiar with the mouse's situation, because in one form or another, issues that seem to threaten our security or happiness have seriously upset us.

The mouse asked the sage to use his mystic powers to prevent the cat from bothering him any longer. The sage responded in an unexpected way by turning the mouse into a cat, and the mouse—who was now a cat—scampered happily away. But after a short time, the cat returned with a new complaint about the dogs that had begun to chase him. Again, he asked for assistance. This time, the sage turned the cat into a dog, and he hurried off with great relief. But almost immediately, the dog found himself harassed by tigers.

Frightened and unhappy, the dog ran back to the sage, complaining that these solutions were not solving the problem, but were actually making the situation worse. He asked for a definitive solution to relieve him of his anxieties. This time, the sage answered his request by transforming the dog into a tiger. But immediately the sage realized his mistake, because the tiger looked at him with a hungry gleam in his eye. Before the tiger could pounce, the sage turned him back into a mouse.

In our own lives, we often imagine that we would be happier in a different environment, only to discover that each circumstance has its own complications. That is the nature of the material world. The wisest solution is to accept our own situation—our own *karma*—with gratitude and to let our experiences become our teacher to help us learn the lessons we need in order to progress.

The Power of False Ego

Like the mouse, many of us do not feel grateful for our difficult experiences, and we do not willingly learn from them. Our false ego stands in the way. The false ego is the aspect of ourselves that believes itself to be the enjoyer, proprietor, and controller of everything, parading about with an inflated sense of its own importance and refusing to surrender to the will of God. As we have just seen, the false ego can cause a lot of trouble and interfere with our spiritual evolution in countless unexpected ways. The *Vedas* teach that false ego is one of the eight material elements that constitute the physical world. These eight elements fall into two categories: gross and subtle. The gross elements are those we would consider physical—earth, water, fire, air, and ether. The subtle elements are psychological, consisting of mind, intelligence and false ego, and are actually known in many traditions as the subtle body. These eight elements function together as temporary coverings over the eternal spirit soul.

According to Vedic teachings, the universe is constructed in such a way that each of these material elements, or coverings, is ten times thicker and more difficult to penetrate than the previous one. This means that the water element is ten times more difficult to get through than the earth element, air is ten times more difficult than water, and so on, all the way up to false ego, which is the most challenging of all to penetrate. It is far more difficult to master false ego than to gain control over the gross physical elements of earth, water, fire, air, or ether.

False ego is extremely clever and takes many forms. For example, sometimes people may adopt an apparently spiritual lifestyle, giving up meat, intoxication, and promiscuity; keeping their body clean; and behaving properly. But nonetheless, they find it essential to display their virtue to everyone. These people are not much fun to be with, because they keep self-righteously reminding us of their superiority: "You're eating white rice? I don't do that!" "How can you use so much sugar? I don't eat anything made with sugar!" Although they may have freed themselves from certain negative behaviors, they still remain under the influence of false ego, which clings to them stubbornly and is difficult to dissolve.

Detachment

Our progress in overcoming false ego will be more genuine and lasting if we develop detachment. *Detachment helps the ego become less dominant.* To accomplish this, as we saw in the previous chapter, we must first learn to master the senses. This means gaining mastery over the gross material influences in our lives so that we can control animalistic tendencies such as our desires to eat too much, sleep too much, or engage in promiscuity. However, a word of caution is in order at this point: we must not rely only on detachment, or we may find the path too difficult. Remember, spiritual life is also about substituting higher forms of pleasure for lower ones.

While detachment is a necessary component in helping us control our gross material desires, once we master these gross desires our task is far from complete—in fact, the difficult work is just beginning. At this point, we must take inventory to discover the more subtle attachments that are still blocking our spiritual advancement. We cannot work on these subtle attachments without help. On our own, we can all too easily delude ourselves into evaluating our behavior in ways that make us feel comfortable. We need feedback and guidance from others to help us root out deeply entrenched patterns. That is why spiritual association is so necessary, providing us with mentors, peers, and friends who can help us grow.

Friends Help Us Evolve

Real friends do not just stroke each other's egos or encourage nonsense, but remind one another about what is most essential. *True friends are those who connect with us spiritually, motivating us to move faster toward the ultimate goal.* Their own examples should remind us of the benefits of remaining faithful to the devotional process.

A great teacher in my spiritual lineage used to say that one who glorifies us is our enemy and one who criticizes us is our friend. The person who glorifies us is implying that we are fine just as we are, whereas the person who criticizes us sees what we need to work on—and, given that we are in the material realm, we all have many areas needing improvement. That is why those who remind us to do more intense work on ourselves are our true friends. We should be cautious when people glorify us too much and, whenever we accomplish anything of merit, we should pass any praise on to the Lord, who allowed us to be used as an instrument in His service. When we start taking credit for our successes, we accept all the other material burdens that come along with such an attitude.

As we release our material attachments, we may want to know how to assess our spiritual progress. One simple way to know we are advancing is to notice whether or not many of our previous activities and environments have become boring or unpleasant. We are making progress when we are no longer excited by the mundane music we used to listen to, the places we used to frequent, or the friends we used to associate with who are still locked into materialistic patterns. Gradually we start feeling drained by such pastimes, environments, and people. This is a sign that something is changing. Although externally we may appear the same as before, inwardly we have become different, because our level of consciousness has become more elevated.

The Dark Night of the Soul

In the process of freeing ourselves from material entanglements, we may experience a "dark night of the soul," which is a period of serious testing. In order to fortify us for such difficult periods, esoteric teachings emphasize the need to be regulated and unaffected by happiness or distress. When we live a regulated life, as we have seen, we develop equipoise and learn to be undisturbed by circumstances. Then when difficulties come, we are prepared.

Surgeons, paramedics, and firefighters are carefully trained for emergencies. When a crisis arises, they know just what to do. A firefighter pulls on boots, slides down the pole, jumps on the truck, turns on the siren, and races off to the fire. A paramedic checks for vital signs and instigates life-saving measures. A surgeon cuts in the proper places and makes the necessary repairs. Because these people are prepared, danger or the sight of blood does not deter them.

However, if we are not trained, or if we are trained improperly, then in an emergency our mind goes blank or panic sets in. We have no idea how to act. Just as the paramedic or firefighter must be trained to act properly in a material emergency, we must also be thoroughly prepared in spiritual life. We must learn ahead of time how to handle the crises that occur because of our desire for sense gratification. If we are well fortified in advance, then when these crises come—and come they will—we will immediately do what is necessary to remain steady and unaffected.

In Sanskrit there is a principle called *akincana*, meaning that the Lord sometimes intervenes in our lives to take everything away. Although we may not understand His reasons at the time, the Lord is actually clearing the path for something greater. We cannot receive His gifts unless we first stop clinging to what we already have; we often need a "divine push" to let go. When this push comes, we may cry out in anguish, "Oh, God, I have nothing!" But we must remember at these times that everything happens for a purpose. If God does not remove our old attachments, He may find our hands too full to receive the blessings He wishes to bestow.

In the streets of our cities we may notice homeless men or women who have almost nothing, but who cling ferociously to the few useless objects they have managed to acquire. These simple possessions are vital for these people, who can become vicious if anyone tries to take them away. Although this behavior may seem absurd, most of us act in just the same way. We are so deeply attached to useless junk that we leave no space for anything of greater value. Some of us must lose everything before we are open to receiving higher blessings.

The dark night of the soul is that period during which everything seems to go wrong even though we have been trying to live a spiritual life. In such circumstances, we may be tempted to think, "Even God does not love me. I'm chanting; I'm praying; I'm meditating; I'm fasting; I'm vegetarian; I'm kind to people; I read the scriptures; I respect the saints; I have a spiritual teacher. I'm doing everything I know how to do, but still the Lord doesn't love me." But if we remain equipoised, this is the point at which our consciousness can genuinely mature. We are no longer seeking material results from our spiritual behavior, because all material rewards have been taken away. If we persevere in our spiritual life despite these difficulties, we are learning to love and serve God no matter what.

Turning Negatives into Positives

The dark night of the soul offers a serious challenge to material consciousness, inviting us to become more transcendental. When we live on a transcendental level, we accept every circumstance as favorable, learning to turn negatives into positives and to make positives even more positive. We can make a negative situation positive by examining it closely, asking ourselves, "Why has this come about? God is all-loving and there are no accidents in the universe. There must be a good reason for this problem to appear in my life." Such an attitude allows an event that might initially seem negative to become a stepping-stone instead. In everyday life, when we climb a set of stairs, we are engaged in a process of confrontation and advancement: first we confront the next step and then we advance to it. Similarly, in spiritual life we cannot experience advancement without confrontation. We cannot go to the next level without tests, just as university students must take examinations at the end of each semester to demonstrate their level of accomplishment to the teacher.

Negative situations provide opportunities for us to prove our readiness—or lack of it—for the next level of spiritual life. Here is a simple example. Imagine that someone said to you, "Your face is so ugly! I can't bear to look at you!" At this point you have a choice. You can react in kind by getting furious, making a threatening gesture and warning that person about the ugly effects of a black eye. Or you can resist reacting and humbly respond, "I am sorry that you are disturbed, but that's your problem." Remember, if we take the statement in a negative way, we actually lower ourselves to the attacker's level. Indeed, if we accept the words as an attack and get caught up in reaction, we are already vanquished because we have lost our self-mastery. Our attacker will harass us even more, until we become trapped in a cycle of negativity.

If others disturb us, we can use the situation as a step in our spiritual development. viewing the confrontation as a test. When we become upset, we are impeding our spiritual progress. In contrast, if we remain unaffected, our would-be attacker will back away and will even feel ridiculous after a while. Not only have we defeated the other person, who has not demonstrated sufficient power to affect us, but we have also helped raise that individual's consciousness.

Spiritual warriors are not merely theoretical lecturers or scholars. First and foremost, they are practitioners. According to their level of realization, practitioners are held accountable for what they do as well as for what they say. Spiritual warriors pay a price if they behave improperly because the angels and demigods monitor their consciousness. For these reasons, simply hearing or reading about spiritual principles is not enough. We must learn to apply them to our own circumstances. Life is very dear, and the way in which we use our time is extremely significant. Spiritual teachings should always have practical applications. We should gain a clear sense of how the principles work so that we can use them in daily life and learn from our experiences how to improve our service to others and to God.

An example from my own experience may help to illustrate this point. Sometimes I present five or six lectures or interviews in one day. Because I give so many programs, I have experienced many different types of interferences and have learned to anticipate such challenges. Recently I was supposed to appear on a television program in Nigeria after a visit to a government official. Since the official could not see us on time, we were delayed and arrived at the television station a bit behind schedule. Despite our lateness we had to wait, because some legal papers had to be arranged. I could have complained, "Oh! This is so terrible. Here I have been delayed by the official, I'm late for this program, and now I'm being kept waiting even longer! I'm just going to leave, because every time I come to this TV station I wind up waiting two to six hours anyway. I'm tired of it!" As a matter of fact, it is true; I have never arrived at that station and been able to go directly on the air.

But why should I be disturbed? Instead, I decided, "Well, here's some extra time for me to catch up on some writing and reading. Or I can take this period to chant and pray, so that when I do appear on the program I can invite the Lord to help me say something to uplift everyone's consciousness." In this way, I did not lose any time, nor did I waste my energy in frustration or anger.

The Importance of Faith

The dark night of the soul can seem interminable. A leap of faith is necessary if we are to weather its challenges successfully. But we must be careful, because faith can function on several different levels. For example, criminals may have firm faith that their next bank robbery will bring them millions of dollars, or investors may choose catastrophic investments based on misplaced faith in the transitory world of the stock market. Although these are examples of faith, obviously the faith is misdirected toward mundane goals rather than spiritual ones.

The idea is to develop strong, properly directed faith based upon the teachings of the saints and scriptures. In saner times, such faith would be strengthened by the examples of our peers in daily life, but in today's society very few people live according to the scriptures. With no ready examples around us, we may devalue spiritual teachings or become frightened of them. This is why we must make a concerted effort to find and associate with other spiritual people. As we witness the positive effects of spiritual life on them, we gain more willingness to imitate their lifestyles.

The scriptures abound with examples of proper spiritual behavior. Unfortunately, although we can gain enthusiasm from these stories, we may still view them as theoretical. We can all too easily dismiss the accomplishments of saintly heroes or heroines by saying, "Well, that's Jesus; that's Moses; that's Buddha; that's Muhammad; that's the *gosvamis*. They are sons of God! Of course I can't be like that." But we are mistaken. Such prophets and teachers have come to show us how to become exactly like them.

Those Christians who consider Jesus to be God may believe they are elevating and respecting Jesus in this way, but actually, they are doing a disservice. Jesus himself says in John 5:30, "I can do nothing on my own authority; as I hear, I judge; and my judgment is just, because I seek not my own will but the will of Him who sent me." He clearly states that he is working on behalf of his Father. By considering Jesus to be God, Christians are justifying the human tendency to err and minimizing the importance of trying to become like Jesus. They can excuse themselves by saying, "After all, Jesus is God, and I am a mere human being." But Jesus reminded us that we could imitate his feats when he said in John 14:12, "Truly, truly, I say to you, he who believes in me will also do the works that I do; and greater works than these will he do."

However, it is also true that in Kali-yuga, or the Age of Quarrel, we cannot easily imitate the saints. Out of His love for us, the Lord complements our efforts because He knows how hard it is in these times to be saintly. He specifically says in the *Bhagavad-gita* 9.22 that He maintains what we have and supplies what we lack:

> *ananyas cintayanto mam*
> *ye janah paryupasate*
> *tesam nityabhiyuktanam*
> *yoga-ksemam vahamy aham*

> *But those who always worship Me with exclusive devotion, meditating on My transcendental form—to them I carry what they lack, and I preserve what they have.*

But His intervention does not come without a price; we still must reach a certain spiritual level and continue to work hard to receive the assistance that is available. Once we have reached that point, the Lord and His agents will seize our hands and pull us up. The Lord's mercy is always greater than His law, and God is constantly considering our mitigating circumstances and extending His loving help.

A Hospital for Our Spiritual Diseases

People who are serious about spiritual life do not seek wealth, fame, or any other type of opulence. But in material life, these goals are exactly what we pursue. Those who are genuinely spiritual, though, will use material gain only to enhance devotional service to the Lord. The proper mood is, "How can I make money so I don't have to worry about money? How can I have enough money to do this project for the Lord?" And if someone on a spiritual path does happen to become famous, that fame can be a vehicle for directing attention to the Lord and His representatives.

Each of us should try to become a dedicated servant, no matter what our outer circumstances. Service is a process of cleansing and healing, just as if we were in a hospital. We take shelter of a spiritual teacher for the same reasons we go to the hospital: because we are sick and recognize that we need help. As patients, we willingly take medication, follow the doctor's orders, and accept the care offered to us in that environment. Because all spiritual people are not exactly the same, there is no single type of illness that afflicts them. Spiritual "diseases" come in a wide variety of forms and intensities. The beauty of the situation is that such persons at least have the chance to recognize the problem and put themselves in the "hospital" for treatment. If they take the spiritual medicine as directed, they will quickly regain their natural healthy state.

But a hospital can also be dangerous, because sometimes people can contract new diseases or infections during their stay. They may enter with one disease and catch something else, falling prey to the innumerable germs concentrated in that environment. In a similar way, while working on ourselves we must be careful not to adopt the bad habits of others around us.

For example, if people who indulge their senses regularly surround us, even in spiritual groups, we may easily become distracted by sense gratification. Or we may become self-centered, taking care of ourselves to the exclusion of anyone else, again following the poor examples of those around us.

In the process of healing, our attitude is critically important, to the extent that two people can be in the same environment and achieve entirely different results according to their mental state. Someone who is morbid, depressed, and dismal will encounter far more difficulties than one who has a vibrant consciousness. Although both may be equally sick at the outset, the more positive, energetic person will make the necessary effort to maintain a constructive attitude. Such an individual will be out of the hospital long before the other.

Become the Lord's Slave and Be Free

Part of our material disease is holding persistently to the belief in our total independence. This is ironic because, although a certain amount of free will is the birthright of all human beings, we are not really free. Our minds are controlled. Every time we turn on the television, listen to the radio, read the newspaper, or interact with social institutions, we are being programmed. As odd as it may seem, to truly free ourselves and to avoid being victimized by old age, disease, death, or any other transitory, unnatural aspects of existence, we must literally become slaves of the Lord.

We create our own pain and suffering by clinging to all kinds of egocentric nonsense. Despite the fact that we are responsible for our unhappiness, if we ask the Lord to help, we often refuse His assistance when it comes. We behave like prisoners who, eager to be released, ask the jailer to open the gate but run immediately back inside when the doors do open. Yet we persist in asking, "When are you going to let me out of here?"

Although the Lord makes all kinds of help available to get us out of this material world once and for all, our insanity drives us to seek temporary gratification instead. Because in modern society the pursuit of material pleasures is accepted as normal—and all around us people are doing little else—we can easily become convinced that the single-minded quest for "the good life" is appropriate human behavior.

Material Concerns Can Be Distractions

Such behavior is decidedly detrimental to spiritual life. As our consciousness advances on the spiritual path, the differences between lust and love become increasingly apparent. When we begin to discover how many of our past actions have been covered by lust, we may look back over our lives with a sense of embarrassment or dismay. We realize that much of our behavior was self-serving, even when we had convinced ourselves that we were helping others. Our consciousness was functioning on a material level rather than on a spiritual one.

In these physical bodies, we are constantly experiencing various types of disturbances that interfere with the natural expression of the soul. Remember, a material body is a prison suit. Some suits may be a little more attractive or a little less confining than others, but they are all the results of our incarceration in this material world. In retrospect, we can understand that we have had to make the best of a bad bargain, trapped in yet another physical body rather than fully alive in a spiritual body.

Anything that does not improve the quality of life or

deepen our wisdom is ultimately a distraction. Frequently, our lives become complicated when we own many material objects. Instead of having fewer problems, we have more. But the issue is our level of attachment to these resources and how we use them. If we remain unattached and offer everything in service to the Lord, then our material assets enhance our ability to live spiritually. If they distract us from an ongoing flow of meditation and service, then they become obstacles that we must overcome.

Our Interaction with Higher Beings

Spiritual life requires a process of purification that allows us to gradually develop contact with the transcendental realm. As mentioned earlier, we do not have to leave this physical body to know that God consciousness is real. We can have a personal relationship with the Lord right here and now, and we can also interact with demigods, archangels, or angels. These experiences are accessible in the immediate present if we develop sufficient consciousness of the higher realms. We are actually in the spiritual kingdom at every moment, although we may not realize it because our spiritual faculties are dormant. The spiritual process is one of "waking up" these faculties so that we can experience the spiritual bliss that has been available all along.

Beings in the invisible realms can have a powerful impact on our lives. According to the *Vedas*, there are 33,000,000 types of demigods, some pious and others impious. Although the impious demigods have a powerful connection to the Lord, they are mischievous or deviant. They resemble people who have been involved in a bona fide spiritual system but have then chosen to turn away. In contrast, the pious demigods are very God conscious and act for the benefit of everyone. In addition to the pious and impious demigods, there are *asuras*, or demons. These demons often have the same powers as the demigods, but they try to bring about chaos in order to destroy God consciousness.

When we examine ancient mythology—Greek, Roman, or Indian, for example—we find that we often dismiss as "myths" those stories about events that are inconceivable to our present levels of understanding. Yet the ideas and themes of these stories about gods and demigods are universal across the traditions, suggesting that at one time there actually were regular interactions between beings on this planet and those in the heavenly kingdoms. But now, as we have seen, the planet has become so thickly covered with mundane collective consciousness that these beings are not eager to come, and many higher beings who once had the assignment to work on this plane no longer do so, preferring a more receptive environment.

Many years ago, my spiritual master was participating in a worship service in Los Angeles. During the *kirtana* or congregational chanting, he started laughing. His disciples later asked him why he had been laughing. Srila Prabhupada replied that Narada Muni, a powerful transcendental being who travels in different universes on behalf of the Lord, had appeared in the midst of the worship service and had also been laughing. Even now such exalted beings occasionally appear if the environment is sufficiently spiritual.[2]

Intense Spiritual Pleasure

In the higher stages of spiritual development, our encounters with the spiritual realm can provide such intense pleasure that the physical body has difficulty containing them. Indeed, the experience of divine love sometimes creates such ecstasy that we can fall into a trance-like state. Even in mundane life, happiness can transform our appearance and behavior. We walk lightly, and we may smile or whistle to such an extent that others may wonder what has happened.

Just imagine a pleasure so powerful that it permeates our consciousness, affecting all the molecules, atoms, and cells in the body. When we are in such a state of ecstasy, we may exhibit unusual symptoms: tears may pour down our cheeks, we may have difficulty speaking, or our hair may stand on end. In such a state, we are simultaneously here and in other dimensions, communicating with the spiritual realms while still in this material body. Such ecstasy is available for everyone, although it is usually heavily covered over. But as soon as we purify and open ourselves, we can behold the blissful reality.

God has no favorites. Everyone has the same chance to become natural, to attain realization, and to experience divine love. It is just a matter of the intensity of our desire to attain these states. As the scriptures remind us, the essential point is to love God with all our hearts and to fully surrender.

Three Requirements for Spiritual Peace

When we experience such love, we attain a deep level of peace. *Bhagavad-gita* 4.39 confirms this with these words:

> *sraddhaval labhate jnanam*
> *tat-parah samyatendriyah*
> *jnanam labdhva param santim*
> *acirenadhigacchati*

A faithful man who is dedicated to transcendental knowledge and who subdues his senses is eligible to achieve knowledge, and having achieved it he quickly attains the supreme spiritual peace.

Three practices—none of which is sufficient alone—are necessary in order to attain this "supreme spiritual peace." As a brief review of some of the points we have discussed so far, let us describe these practices. They can serve as reminders of how to maintain a path of steady, committed spiritual development.

1. *We must have faith.* Sometimes we are embarrassed by the necessity for faith, but we should remember that it is implicit in everything we do. Think about it. When we walk, we have faith that our legs will move. When we eat a meal, we have faith that our body will digest the food. When we go to sleep, we have faith that we will wake up again. We do not need to apologize about the importance of faith. But we must learn to invest our faith wisely. If we make an intelligent investment by placing our faith in spiritual realities, we will obtain positive results. But if we invest poorly by concentrating on the transitory aspects of existence, we will become sad and disappointed, having failed to honor our birthright.

2. *Keep the mind properly absorbed in transcendental knowledge.* When we do so, we are less affected by the impermanence and suffering of the material world. It is important to note, however, that the knowledge must be transcendental, beyond this material realm, not just relative or transitory. To gain exposure to such knowledge, we can read scriptures; perform worship; chant, meditate and pray; attend lectures; listen to tapes; and associate with others who have similar interests.

3. *Regulate the senses.* As explained earlier, this is the key to conquering lust. Without mastery of the senses, we will simply act spontaneously, emotionally, and erratically. Our control of the senses is intimately related to our control of the mind. Remember the old saying, "An idle mind is the devil's workshop." The way in which we fix the mind determines whether we master the senses or are controlled by them, and whether the mind serves the intelligence and the soul, or interferes with their development.

These three practices, executed under proper leadership and guidance, can guarantee anyone full success. Spiritual life is about developing sufficient mastery to put an end to our imprisonment in this material world. That is why spiritual practices aim to regulate the senses, put the mind under control, and allow the intelligence to be stimulated by the soul. The soul is completely cognizant of our relationship to the Godhead. As soon as the mind stops its interference, we naturally overflow with realization and the higher pleasures of eternity and bliss.

Questions and Answers

Question: You once said that we should not go off by ourselves and live as hermits. Since we must remain in this material world, what should we do to counteract the many negative influences in our environments?

Answer: Going off to the Himalayas or to a monastery is neither bad nor good; it is a matter of what you do when you are there. If your body is sitting in a cave, but your mind is constantly thinking about mocha fudge ice cream or your friends at the disco, you might as well be back in the city. But if you can perform genuine service by retiring from the world—if that is your nature and your mission—then that is all right.

Two major categories of spiritual practitioners exist. Those in one category keep to themselves and do not interact with the public, rarely even taking disciples. The other type moves about in the secular world, teaching, sharing, and helping. Particularly in this Age of Quarrel, society has a special need for healthy role models. That is why people in spiritual life should make themselves available to others.

Another problem for those who live in spiritual seclusion is the ease with which they can delude themselves into believing that they are stronger than they actually are. How do they know that they have mastered a situation unless they are in an environment that puts them to the test? To be absorbed in mystical intoxication is not necessarily a sign of advancement. Spiritual maturity exists when we can maintain our higher consciousness regardless of the distractions or obstacles that confront us.

Question: When you talk about sense gratification, I realize that one of the pleasures I am most addicted to is sleep. What is the value of sleep?

Answer: We can serve the Lord even while we are asleep. When we consider that the average person spends about one-third of life sleeping, we can understand the importance of using even that time to learn more about the Lord and to serve Him. Actually, spiritually advanced beings do not sleep as we know it. While their bodies are at rest, they move into different environments—even different universes—to engage in a higher level of service than they perform on the physical level. As we evolve more spiritually, we discover that when the physical body is inactive at night, the subtle body and the soul have even more chance to do service without the restrictions imposed on the physical body.

Before we take rest at night, we should fill our minds with the consciousness of devotion. At least fifteen minutes before we go to sleep—half an hour if possible—we should take the time to read something spiritual or to do some chanting. Before doing so, we must bring closure to what has happened during the day, and deliberately enter another part of our life.

When we retire for the night with a sense of enthusiasm for the adventures that await us and for the services we can perform in the inner realms, we know that the physical body is gradually becoming more spiritualized and less of an obstacle to our spiritual development. On the other hand, if we discover that in the subtle, inner realms our minds are just trying to carry out the desires of the physical body by manipulating material energies, then we need to do more work to align the mind and the intelligence with the soul.

Question: Can you say more about the dark night of the soul? I have been in the middle of one for quite some time, and I would like to gain greater understanding of what it means.

Answer: In spiritual life, the dark night of the soul can occur when we become strong in devotional practice and are extremely determined to serve God. Actually, such a situation often indicates that we have reached a point where we are being prepared for a major positive transition leading to a deeper connection with the Lord.

As we go through this dark period, we must examine our desires and motives to discover the real basis of our spiritual life. When everything is taken away, it becomes easier to see the truth about ourselves. Are we genuinely ready for deeper levels of spiritual realization? Are we really motivated by love of God, or are we just seeking a particular boon from the Lord? The difficulties that arise can help us identify our real platform.

We may discover that we want to receive the tiniest favorable sign, or perhaps even to be chastised, just to know that God is still there. Some people pray at times like this, saying, "If there is a God, then let me see Him now," or, "I'll give it one or two more weeks, and if the situation doesn't change, then I'm not going to stay with God." They think that spiritual life is cheap. For them, God is just an order-taker who should fulfill their demands.

Unless we are properly guided by a spiritual mentor and have reinforcement from a proper spiritual community, we can easily give up when we are going through a dark night of the soul. From a logical perspective we have every reason to abandon our spiritual quest, but we must not do so. Instead, we should say, "No! I have given my entire life to the Lord. Dear Lord, do with me as You like. If it gives You pleasure to keep me in this state of upheaval, then that will be my joy!"

Chapter 5

Sexuality in Everyday Life

Since today's society does not properly understand the difference between love and sex, many of us do not acknowledge the importance of the soul in male-female relationships. Promiscuity is widespread. As we have seen, many leaders are losing influence and power because of poor control of their sexual energy. Families, the basic building blocks of a nation, are unstable and crumbling. Countless unwanted children are born every day.

Sexuality is a powerful life force that is neither inherently good nor bad. Like a knife, its value depends upon how it is used. A doctor can use a knife to save someone's life, or a criminal can use the same knife to kill. The difference lies in the consciousness of the person handling the knife. Similarly, sexuality has two polarities. Sexual activity can be a vehicle for gross abuse, exploitation, and lust. In such circumstances, sex becomes a matter of selfishness. On the other hand, if the sexual act is an exchange of love according to religious principles, it becomes selfless and divine.

Importance of Deep Relationships

Society is in desperate need of deep, loving relationships—far deeper and more loving than are the norm today. We are too distracted by sexual stimulation, viewing each other primarily as sex machines and thereby losing access to a more meaningful and fulfilling level of contact. In most cases, what we normally call love is an arrangement to get some egocentric gratification. Remember, most people have not experienced genuine love. In fact, many of us have been unable to accept expressions of love from anyone—whether parent, friend, or spouse—without wondering about that person's ulterior motives. We have not experienced selfless and unconditional love, and we surely have not found love through sex.

Men and women must become more sophisticated about relationships. This does not necessarily mean that they should abstain from sex. But instead of grasping at fleeting pleasures, they should learn the meaning of commitment and seek to develop strong, enduring, caring connections with each other.

Beauty Comes from the Soul

This society dedicates an inordinate amount of energy to beautifying the body to attract members of the opposite sex. However, it is the soul, not the body, which is the source of our beauty and attractiveness to others. Because God is beautiful, the more we become godly and divine, the more our natural beauty radiates. Sometimes we forget this truth and maintain our relationships at a mere physical level.

But men and women can develop deeper connections with one another. Beyond the physical dimension, women often fall in love and interact with men from the heart, while men frequently relate from the mind. Because of these differences, they often do not understand each other well. Yet there is a still deeper level of relating where these differences dissolve in the radiant energy of the soul. This is when sexuality can become a powerful, constructive force.

Sex Is Sacred

Sex is healthy and natural, and fulfills a divine function. *In its highest form of expression, a sexual relationship means that a man and woman come together in order to serve God, creating an environment for a new soul to enter this material realm and develop its relationship with Him.* When we genuinely view sex as a sacred trust and service, it becomes a spiritual act.

On the other hand, when we consider relationships from a superficial perspective, indulging ourselves in "one-night stands," we are accepting a materialistic, selfish view of human life. A more spiritual cosmology sees human beings as part of a larger community in which each person plays a responsible role. A man who simply impregnates a woman and abandons her is not even demonstrating personal responsibility, much less social responsibility or spiritual understanding. To be socially responsible, a person must be concerned about the welfare of the entire community.

Nowadays many of us engage in sex so frequently that

our sexual vitality has become weak, and many relationships are even failing physically because people cannot satisfy each other. An enormous amount of energy is required to produce semen. Considering that most men and women waste this precious resource, it is no wonder that we are becoming so impotent as a society. Our memories are becoming dull and our ability to fulfill each other on all levels is deteriorating. We are becoming increasingly mechanical in our activities, unable to appreciate deeper levels of association, love, or service.

The Power of Sexual Energy

Sexual energy is the most powerful energy we have. In order to grow spiritually, we must learn to master it. Despite this society's emphasis on sexual activity, underneath it all everyone simply wants to give and receive love, not lust. When we express our sexuality with love, we can raise our level of consciousness; but when we are under the sway of lust, sexuality can lower our consciousness. We can become divine beings or mindless beasts.

Our failure to understand the spiritual aspects of sexuality and procreation has become a serious problem. Gradually the planet is becoming overpopulated with lower-level beings, simply because people engage in sexual activity without being accountable. Self-centered persons who use others as pleasure units cannot expect to give birth to selfless, compassionate, devoted souls. How can such unions produce anything divine? No highly evolved soul would be attracted to such a situation.

We must all be more thoughtful about our sexual conduct. We can easily become distracted by material comforts, and even by sex life itself, to the point that we forget about the importance of genuine love. We must learn to be more loving to one another and more skilled at developing strong, lasting relationships. An enduring relationship, in the form of a committed, loving marriage, provides an invaluable opportunity for a man and a woman to express their sexuality in a spiritual context.

Sexuality in Marriage

In a marriage, husbands and wives should view their partners as gifts from God. Spouses who think in this way, understanding that the Lord has entrusted someone to their care, will be careful to treat their partners in a nurturing manner that pleases the Lord. Marriages established and maintained on such a foundation are extremely loving and sweet, and the children of such a union grow up in a wonderfully supportive atmosphere.

When the couple does join in sexual union, both parties should want the encounter and consider it divine. The experience then becomes an inspiring, profound expression of love. Each time they come together, the man and woman should remember that the ultimate expression of sexuality is the birth of a child. For this reason, they should not use contraceptives or resort to abortion, because these are interferences with the sacred purpose of sexuality.

Contraception is not natural, although it is an accepted practice today. We must be careful not to confuse sociological considerations with spiritual ones. A man and a woman may not want to conceive a child because they lack the financial means to support a new family member, or because they do not feel psychologically ready. But these circumstances are different from the spiritual realities of the situation. Spiritually, when a man and a woman give themselves to each other in sexual union, they must be ready for the natural consequences. Their spiritual consciousness should take priority, guiding them to understand the use of contraceptives from a spiritual perspective rather than a material one.

The Science of Procreation

There is a science about sex life known to ancient civilizations that explains how and when to come together sexually. *The consciousness of the man and the woman during the sexual act has a powerful influence on the soul that eventually comes into the world.* People who engage in sex in a negative state of consciousness produce beings of lower consciousness.

Often today, people have sex under highly unfavorable circumstances—in the dark, while they are intoxicated, or with someone else's spouse. Sometimes the woman may not want to become pregnant, so that even if she does not have an abortion and ultimately gives birth to the baby, the soul of the unwanted child will not be of the highest caliber. Moreover, the baby may come into an environment where the parents neglect it. Such a soul enters this world in a state of crisis.

But if the partners are willing to accept the responsibility involved, and prepare themselves spiritually for the sexual encounter, their consciousness actually summons a higher soul who can make a positive contribution to the world. We must never forget that the child's future depends, to a greater extent than we may realize, upon the parents' consciousness at the time of conception. A man and woman engaging in sexual activity are accepting a sacred trust.

A man and a woman who are ready to conceive a child should make special efforts to create a peaceful, spiritual environment before engaging in sex. They can chant, meditate, read spiritual literature, and generally prepare their consciousness to welcome a highly evolved soul. Even during pregnancy, the future parents must create a healthy, loving, supportive atmosphere for their offspring. Remember, the soul begins its education as soon as it enters the womb. Modern science is just beginning to confirm this, discovering that the fetus is conscious and can learn while developing inside the mother. The sounds that it hears, the food the mother consumes, the atmosphere that surrounds the mother—all these factors and many others affect the child's consciousness long before it is born.

Natural Sexuality

From what we have said up to this point, it must be apparent that the most natural situation in a marriage is for the husband and wife to engage in sexual activity only when they wish to conceive a child. This ensures that the partners are ready to be accountable and responsible for what they produce. Marriages should function as closely to this ideal as possible, but the spouses must always decide between themselves how totally they can observe such a sexual discipline.

Actually, a husband and wife who engage in sex life only for purposes of procreation are practicing a form of celibacy. In one sense, it is even greater celibacy than avoiding contact with the opposite sex altogether, because it can require stronger sense control. We should remember that the more we please the Lord by using the body, mind, and intelligence in ways that He intended, the faster we can escape from the prison of this material world. On the other hand, if we continue to play the "body game," interfering with the body's natural functioning, then we will have to take repeated births until we can transcend our desire for material sense gratification.

How a Soul Chooses its Circumstances

Although earlier we described the ways in which a soul seeking birth can try to select potential parents, the choice of birth circumstances is not just up to the future child. Both the child and the parents participate in deciding when and where the child will come into the world. The mentality of two specific parents attracts a certain type of soul and, conversely, a particular type of soul is drawn to certain parents, an arrangement which the demigods help to facilitate.

Keep in mind that *karma* is quite exacting. For example, if someone robs a bank, it is by karmic arrangement that one particular bank is robbed rather than another. Also, *karma* dictates who will be in the bank at that particular time. All of these events are being minutely adjusted according to the *karma* of those involved.

You may ask, "Do you mean that it was my desire and my attitude that produced this deformed child?" Not necessarily. It may be that you need to experience such a situation as a parent for further spiritual growth. Or this particular child may require just such a deformity, and just such a parent as you, in order to progress to the next level of unfoldment. All of these circumstances are exactingly adjusted. This does not mean that we should be indifferent to each others' difficulties, but we must remember that these physical lifetimes are short chapters in the existence of each soul.

In addition to the efforts of the potential parents and child to choose the proper situation for an upcoming birth, there is another factor at work. The soul does not actually arrange for its situation in life directly. Ultimately, higher authorities working on behalf of the Lord create all of the relevant circumstances. These authorities establish physical traits such as our nose, the color of our eyes, the color of our hair, or our body type, and environments such as our siblings, our mother, or our nationality. Working with what we might call the "karmic board," they ensure that everything is arranged in proper alignment for the soul taking birth. All these arrangements are part of the experience that the soul has chosen by being attracted to the consciousness of the parents.

Karma and Free Will

Remember, there are no accidents in the universe. God does not make mistakes and He is not unfair. The situations in which we find ourselves, including those with our mates as well as with our children, have arisen for specific reasons. We should learn to inquire into what these reasons might be, so that we may learn our lessons and take the appropriate actions.

Often, it may seem that we are being moved about like tiny pawns on a giant chessboard. But we still have free will, because everything is happening according to our desire. When we add together all the notions about what we want, taking into account the past as well as the present, we get an overall result that will determine the arrangements that the demigods and their agents need to make for us. In other words, the sum total of our desires determines our circumstances. That is why we must be careful about how we direct our energies. The universe offers us more of anything to which we give our concentrated attention.

We must accept responsibility for all the patterns in our lives, whether we are happy with them or not. Just like a customer in a restaurant, we may not like the way a particular soup tastes, but we still recognize that we ordered that soup and that we will have to pay for it. By being accountable, we can gain the power to make a change.

The Practice of Celibacy

Although sexuality, expressed in a regulated, spiritually oriented way, is appropriate for most people, important exceptions exist. Every culture has special spiritual practices that convey unusual powers. One of these practices is celibacy, which can help a person develop a strong, focused love for all living beings. Celibate individuals, instead of being limited to one relationship, are able to offer deep love and concern to anyone who comes into their environment.

The principle of celibacy lies at the inner core of many religions. The New Testament, in I Corinthians 7, teaches us that it is best to be celibate. However, this same chapter tells us that it is preferable to marry than to burn with desire. The whole idea behind celibacy is that we must feel a specific calling to this way of life, at which point we can learn from esoteric spiritual knowledge about its meaning and practice.

Many techniques are available to allow us to conserve sexual energy to further our spiritual advancement and service. For example, if one preserves the tremendous vital energy contained in even one drop of semen and channels it upward, this energy can elevate one's consciousness. However, a word of caution: men and women should have a specific "calling" to a celibate way of life before engaging in any such practices. In addition, they should be careful not to practice celibacy in isolation, without loving associations. If they are going to exist without an immediate partner, they must learn to see everyone as their family and surround themselves with loving relationships.

Actually, celibacy is quite rare, and we do not recommend it for most people. As a general rule, society requires strong, God conscious families, which is why most people should marry and raise healthy children instead of practicing celibacy. But everyone should understand that certain individuals choose a celibate lifestyle in order to develop superhuman powers to serve others in a most dedicated, loving way.

At the same time, we must remember that our culture overemphasizes the role of sexuality and that love does not necessarily begin or end with sexual intercourse. This does not mean that sex cannot be part of a loving relationship between husband and wife. It is a matter of maintaining a healthy balance between sexual expression and other aspects of life. The important point is that people should not miss the experience of higher love because they are focusing only on the physical body.

In the presence of celibate persons, we often experience intense levels of vitality and love. Genuinely celibate people have an aura around them, because they have powerful energies of selfless compassion that they freely share with others. Priests in ancient Egypt and other early civilizations knew this fact quite well, and many practitioners in modern India still do. Their celibacy empowers them to accomplish amazing feats. Mahatma Gandhi was an example of this phenomenon; he derived much of his strength from his celibacy.

Paradoxically, many celibate individuals are extremely attractive to members of the opposite sex. This is because of the powerful love such people can radiate. There is nothing wrong with this; attraction is natural between the sexes. But the celibate person's responsibility is to be completely unselfish and totally concerned about others. The true celibate has union with others from the heart and not through genitalia.

Celibacy Is Not Denial

When properly understood and practiced, celibacy is not a matter of self-denial. It is a question of love. Individuals who become celibate in order to dedicate their energies to God's service do not experience celibacy as a sacrifice. Their sexual energy transforms itself into selfless compassion and devotion, which they distribute widely to everyone they encounter. They view themselves first and foremost as servants of God and society, always seeking to be channels for divine energies to heal, guide, or encourage others.

Celibacy is appropriate only if we choose it freely. If we try to suppress our sexual desire without having focused it in a different direction, we may discover within ourselves a tremendous false ego, intense anger, or tendencies to be surprisingly destructive. *We must learn to redirect our sexual energy instead of denying its existence or hoping it will go away.* False celibacy simply becomes another unnatural distortion of our sexuality, destroying our society even further.

Celibacy should never be a matter of running away from a condition we cannot face. For example, some people deprive themselves of contact with members of the opposite sex because they are not able to cope with their own sexuality. The remedy to this situation is greater self-knowledge, not avoidance.

Nor should celibacy be dictated from outside. When it is, we can develop strange, unnatural behaviors. From a practical perspective, it is easy to understand why certain religious institutions impose the practice of celibacy upon its priests. Those in positions of leadership can easily exploit the opposite sex. Without some form of restraint, a priest in frequent contact with women about confidential matters could easily succumb to sexual temptation. But unfortunately, when celibacy is externally imposed, many priests often long for sexual contact and find illicit ways to fulfill their desires.

Every action is linked to our wish for pleasure, and our desire for pleasure originates with our sexual energy. When we are not highly attuned, we seek fulfillment in the form of exploitation and selfish gratification. Therefore, if we lack the genuine desire to be celibate, which can be the case, for example, if others impose celibacy upon us; if we are impotent; or if we are afraid to express our sexuality, the practice of celibacy can be harmful. We will only experience frustration and anger, because we are depriving ourselves of pleasures that we deeply long for. By forcing ourselves to be celibate in such circumstances, we may be doing violence to ourselves and, ultimately, to others. We are not experiencing a "higher taste," but merely causing more suffering in the world.

Renunciation Takes Various Forms

True celibacy, then, is a form of renunciation in favor of a higher good. Instead of being a matter of denial or avoidance, renunciation is a question of how available we make ourselves for God's service. For each person, renunciation can take a different form suited to that individual's particular development. For example, those accustomed to the bustle of outer activity may find that renunciation requires them to withdraw and do less.

But for those attached to being alone, renunciation might mean taking on more external involvements, activities, and relationships. The love of solitude may be a form of sense gratification, which is a weakness. Interactions with others may reveal that they are not nearly as detached from the world as they would like to think, because their ascetic lifestyle has become a buffer to protect them from genuine engagement in life.

Many *yogis* who engage in their meditation under a tree, in a cave, or in the mountains would fall apart if they had to maintain daily contact with other people. In addition, we have all heard of *swamis* or *gurus* who, after spending years in the Himalayas, started making teaching tours to Europe or America, where they eventually fell from their exalted position and succumbed to temptation.

The real test of renunciation comes as we encounter various situations in daily life. Renunciation means a genuine commitment to serve the Lord rather than ourselves in all circumstances. We must see ourselves as caretakers for the Lord rather than proprietors of anyone or anything. However, renunciation does not mean being impersonal or indifferent to relationships. On the contrary, it actually means being more caring, attentive, sharing, aware, and protective—not because we are attached to our own fulfillment, but because we are making an offering to the Lord. What we are renouncing is the ascendancy of the false ego, which keeps us imprisoned in this material world.

Celibacy in Marriage

Celibacy is not just for priests and other religious leaders. Earlier we mentioned that engaging in marital sex only for purposes of procreation could be considered a form of celibacy. In the form of complete abstinence from sexual activity for a period of time, celibacy can play another important role in marriage. Sometimes relationships can become difficult because the people see each other only on the physical level. In such circumstances there may be advantages to completely abstaining from any form of sexual activity.

For example, a couple could mutually agree to be celibate for five or six months in order to give themselves the space to experience each other in a different way. A break from their usual sexual routine may give them the opportunity to deepen and strengthen other aspects of their relationship. Eventually, they may find that many of their problems resolve themselves with very little deliberate effort.

Placing Material Life in Perspective

Ultimately, each of us must learn to be free by mastering our senses and desires within the constraints imposed by these physical bodies in this material world. Whether we are celibate or sexually active, we should always connect with something higher that will guide us, protect us, enliven us, and give us a sense of security. The ancient Vedic teachings remind us, as do many other traditions, that all material and spiritual worlds originate in God. Therefore, if we try to please the Lord, we are automatically in touch with the nucleus of everything. Then whatever we need will come to us naturally.

Unfortunately, most of us ignore this fact and head in the wrong direction. Instead of improving our relationship with the Lord, we spend most of our time trying to satisfy our lower desires. Sexuality, if misunderstood, can be a trap to keep us ensnared in the material world. Certainly we must pay attention to the body in order to function effectively. But if our priorities are sense gratification and self-satisfaction above all else, we will have to keep returning to the physical world to play the sensual and material games over and over again. On the other hand, if spiritual life is our commitment, then our experiences in this world will not be ends in themselves, but will be signposts pointing the way back home to God.

Questions and Answers

Question: I have been practicing celibacy for about two years. At first I forced myself, and I struggled for a while. But now I am grateful, because I know who I am. I'm in a position now to draw a person to me I really like, because I see relationships from a spiritual point of view. But what about a married person who has satisfied the need for children? Is it natural for that person to not have sexual desire?

Answer: It is wonderful that you have been able to practice celibacy and learn so much from it. As we just mentioned, celibacy can allow you to develop deeper relationships. Also, people do not realize that promiscuous sex actually causes you to age faster. Men expend a great amount of vital energy just to produce one drop of semen. Many years ago when Muhammad Ali was the world heavyweight champion, I made myself available to him as a consultant. He liked to introduce me as

"Swami, my friend the celibate monk." Once, in appreciation of my vow of celibacy, he explained that his trainer always told him to abstain from sex for three or four months before he went into a major fight. Many athletes know that sexual activity can lower their resistance, their perceptiveness, and their ability to function.

As for the level of sexual desire in marriage, it is generally different for men than for women. Although men may not want to admit it, a woman can be much more sexually powerful than a man. But at the same time, her sexuality is expressed in many different ways. For example, she can transform her sexual energy into love for her children, or into an affectionate relationship with her husband based on touching, holding hands, or saying kind words. She is still expressing her sexual energy, but in other forms.

On the other hand, a man has a greater desire for the actual physical act. So a couple must engage in honest discussion and evaluation in order to work the situation out. Just keep in mind that losing one's drive for sexual activity is not unnatural; on the contrary, it can be healthy.

Question: I was having a discussion with a friend of mine who was talking about getting artificially inseminated. What are the consequences of artificial insemination?

Answer: There are many consequences. The major consequence is that the mother and child may have no idea of the connection between that particular sperm and the man who donated it—the child's biological father. What is it like to carry a child without having any idea who the father is? What is it like to have no chance of ever knowing your father? It is similar to adoption. We may adopt a child and not know who the mother or father is, yet the man and woman who actually conceived the child exert a powerful influence on that child's personality.

This is similar to the situation in modern medicine in which the recipient of a heart transplant, or of some other vital organ, often picks up distinct personality traits from the donor. These medical procedures are not as simple as most people think. The influence of the donor definitely exists.

If, knowing all these facts, we are ready to take the consequences of our decision, then artificial insemination may be all right. But we should be aware of the many ramifications.

Question: Is there any merit to the various spiritually oriented sexual practices that use the sexual act for yogic purposes to raise consciousness? Can these be morally acceptable in a situation without the anticipation of childbirth?

Answer: Many are familiar with Tantra and its science of controlling sexual energy to experience higher consciousness during the sex act itself. Unfortunately, these days, many people who practice Tantra are just engaging in illicit affairs under the label of spirituality. But serious practitioners realize that the essence of Tantra is to understand the value of the feminine and masculine polarities—the yin and the yang—and to realize the actual significance of the life force.

We must remember that the bona fide tantric systems, which emphasize reaching superconsciousness through sexual union, are based on control of sexual energy, not promiscuous sexual expression. This simple fact indicates the power inherent in sexuality. Tantric sex is a highly regulated practice that confines the sexual energy for a certain period of time. In this restriction and channeling of sexual energy, Tantra is similar to celibacy.

We must also understand the difference between using sexual techniques to gain mystic power and engaging in sex as an expression of love and devotion. The left-handed sides of Tantra, witchcraft, and many other black arts, rely on practices opposed to spiritual alignment, frequently turning traditional spiritual knowledge upside down. These practices are derived from the knowledge that sexual energy in itself is neutral. When properly directed, it is a catalyst for love and ecstasy. But in its demonic form, sexual energy can express itself as promiscuity or be used to gain dominance over others. We are on dangerous ground if we want to harness sexual energy for the power it gives us rather than for love and procreation.

Earlier in our history, spiritual life was considered natural. Indeed, even today we do not have to know many deep laws and principles to be spiritual. We simply need to understand what is genuinely natural and base our behavior on that knowledge. Any attempt on our part to interfere with or reject the normal outcome of the sexual act means we are going against the order of the universe. We must be ready for the consequences of such actions.

Chapter 6

Love Between a Man and a Woman

Love is necessary for good health. *Someone who is not part of a loving relationship is ten times more likely to experience chronic disease, and five times more likely to have a mental breakdown than someone who is.* Obviously, love is not just an essential element in higher spiritual experiences, but it is also a fundamental necessity for physical survival and well-being.

For many of us, love finds meaningful expression in a relationship with someone of the opposite sex. The relationship between a man and a woman is the foundation of the family unit, which is in turn the bedrock of society, nations, and the world order. If we do not learn how to create stronger, more positive male-female relationships, we are inviting even greater confusion around the planet.

Lack of Depth in Today's Society

Modern society is extremely impersonal. Our mechanized and electronic world keeps us apart from one another as we drive our automobiles, watch our televisions, sit in front of our computers, and work in our sealed offices far from home. Many people prefer to spend their time playing with toys instead of developing genuine, deep, heart-to-heart relationships. Since so many material conveniences exist in the marketplace to use as we see fit, we have learned to view them as objects dedicated to our own pleasure. Unfortunately, we have developed the habit of viewing other people in the same way. The result is tremendous competition, anxiety, and neediness. Believing that true love is fiction, many of us give up the search for a genuine lover and settle for a relationship of convenience.

Our society is full of people whose paranoia and fear of failure prevent them from having deep relationships. Many suffer because they are unable to attain a sense of genuine well-being. As they go about their daily activities, they share this unhappy mentality with others. Consequently, disillusionment and cynicism become widespread.

The influence of modernity, which minimizes the importance of accountability and commitments, is one of the reasons that couples are experiencing more difficulties in their marriages. Everything is constantly changing at such a rapid pace, which is a prominent characteristic of the twenty-first century. This unconsciously causes many people to feel comfortable when they also change their partners or spouses. For instance, the average person in America changes cars every three or four years and houses every seven years. Furthermore, during their lifetime, they change professions about three or four times, jobs about ten times, and lose their jobs seven times. With the massive gathering of data, the amount of total information available to us is doubling every one or two years.

Furthermore, almost one-third of all married Americans have had an affair.[3] However, only nine percent of men and six percent of women plan to marry the person with whom they had an unfaithful relationship.[4] And more than half of those who do marry that partner later divorce. Surely the constant bombardment of pornography adds to this problem. According to *U.S. News and World Report*, there were 40,000 sex-oriented websites on the Internet in 2000 and the number is growing everyday.[5] No wonder recent surveys report that the average American male thinks of sex once every thirty minutes. And most of the thoughts focus more on genitality rather than on sexuality, meaning that they focus more on the stimulation of the genitals rather than on healthy sexual relationships.

Only in the last 150 years has there been more of a focus on erotic and romantic love, rather than on responsibility. Leo Tolstoy has drawn attention to the difference between so-called "being in love" and "loving." Most people's idea of love is self-centered rather than selfless, unconditional love. Unconditional love is given to us in many traditions. In Christianity, it is know as "agape;" in Confucianism, it is referred to as "universal love;" in Buddhism, it is referred to as "*metta;*" and in Hinduism, it is referred to as "*bhakti.*" These words refer to the real love that we are all starving for. Life, being a school of love, is trying to prepare us distinctly for this unconditional spiritual love.

Marianne Williamson explains that a holy relationship involves honesty and will lead to healing. However, an erotic relationship will be filled with dishonesty, and we will hide our weaknesses. When people marry, they should not marry to escape the world, but to see how to heal it. We should even be able to love our enemies so that we will have no enemies. These days, due to the intense focus on erotic love, partners who thought they were "in love" turn on each other and become each other's worst enemies. When we have a divinely focused relationship, partners come together to share joy and enlightenment. But in a relationship dominated by the false ego, the partners come together to share desperation.

Loving Others Means Loving Ourselves

We obviously cannot heal the world if we are too wounded ourselves. The first love affair we must successfully consummate is with ourselves. No one has the power to make someone else love him or her, but each person can always give away love. As we have already said, love is a decision that we can personally make at any time and under any circumstance. As we draw upon the divine energy of God and as we really love Him, then we can authentically love others. We should not expect love to descend on us like an attack of epilepsy. Love is really the energy of the soul; therefore, when we are asking for love, we are asking for a connection with the soul, which is part and parcel of the Godhead. Therefore, real love between partners is the hunger and energy of the soul trying to connect with the Lord by trying to connect with another soul. When a man and a woman come together, they fulfill their purpose by reminding each other how to dive deeper into the bliss of the spiritual journey. Let us remind ourselves that we are always in love with God and the whole creation; we have just allowed lust to cover this truth over.

People who do not love themselves cannot love others. Anyone looking for a mate should ascertain whether the potential partner has a healthy sense of self-love. People who behave destructively toward themselves cannot love others, and they carry their negative feelings into their relationships. How can such a person make a deep connection with someone else? In particular, people who engage in obviously harmful activities such as taking drugs, becoming intoxicated, compulsively gambling, or indulging in illicit sex are doing a disservice to themselves, and will share these degrading habits with others.

A profound loving relationship with such a person is not possible. If we believe anything to the contrary, we are indulging in wishful thinking. Individuals who lack self-love cannot share deeply with others because they only have access to the most superficial aspects of themselves. We must keep our eyes open when seeking a partner. If we are frantically searching for someone, we are likely to paint our own images on anyone who comes our way. The object of our fantasy will appear to possess the most wonderful qualities because, after all, we painted the picture. In such cases, we fall in love with our own conceptions rather than genuinely caring about the other person.

How could we ever be so foolish? Actually, it is very easy. Unaware that our actual wholeness is accessible internally, we simply find someone who outwardly conforms to our idea of an attractive person, and use that individual as a screen upon which to project our fantasies in the form of hopes, fears, and desires.

This process of externalization and projection usually lies at the origin of romantic love, and the romance endures only as long as the illusion remains intact. Often the relationship disintegrates because the person is not at all what we anticipated. We may initially conclude, "Oh, I'm in love! This is the one I've been waiting for." But after some time we realize that we were merely intoxicated with our own ideas, which prevented us from acknowledging what we really knew all along: that this person is not the one for us.

The Quest for Wholeness

Men and women pursue each other in their quest for wholeness. The male, lacking some basic feminine traits, seeks a woman who can give him what he needs. Actually, he is looking for the woman missing within himself. Similarly, the female is seeking outside herself for the masculine aspect lying dormant within her.

We all have within us a certain degree of imbalance between our masculine and feminine qualities. Becoming whole means establishing equilibrium between them. The more we are willing to value a woman's authentic masculine side and a man's genuine feminine side, the healthier our relationships will be. As we become balanced and complete unto ourselves, we can more easily attract a similarly balanced and complete partner to assist us in our service.

When two incomplete personalities come together, the result is not wholeness, but greater frustration. *Two needy people cannot make each other happy. They are too busy trying to find fulfillment for themselves.* When we become too desperate about anything, we should be careful. As long as we believe that someone "out there" will make us happy, we will never be successful in any relationship. But when we gain access to deeper layers of ourselves, we attain more of our natural harmony with nature and with the Supreme Personality of Godhead. Then we become more complete and have a greater balance of masculine and feminine energies.

Two whole personalities who come together have the

opportunity to develop a strong relationship. They are not excessively dominant or dependent, nor do they manipulate each other to shore up their own insecurities. Such people do not behave like beggars, looking for someone to rob or to perform miracles for them. Even if they ultimately fail to attract a partner, they will not feel lost, because they appreciate everything that the Lord has done for them. Instead of trying to acquire something for themselves, they will want to share their wholeness with others. In such a state they come to resemble— in their own small way—the reservoir of divinity, the Supreme Personality of Godhead, who radiates love to everyone.

The more we are whole, the more we are naturally loving and capable of divine associations because, in our essence, we are actually loving beings who are only temporarily covered over. We begin to experience greater wholeness as we understand our inner nature as spirit souls and experience our connection with the Lord.

However, in our quest for wholeness, we must be careful not to believe that we are healthier and more balanced than others. Remember, we are all insane to have taken birth in these material bodies in the first place. This limited physical world is largely one of frustration, depression, anxiety, and gloom, in which we live from day to day longing for the pleasure and ecstasy we know are available somewhere. We ask frantically, "Where is that love?" Lonely and depressed, we know something is wrong with us because we just cannot seem to find what we are seeking.

Distorted Gender Roles

We have seen that every person is a combination of

masculine and feminine elements in differing proportions. This fact is apparent even on a physiological level: the body of every male contains female hormones, and female bodies contain male hormones. Women have breasts, as do men, and for all their differences, the reproductive organs are alike in many ways.

Modern sinful culture forces us into an artificially distorted role-play between the sexes. A man is afraid to be sensitive, compassionate, or caring, but because he does not develop the gentle side of himself, he does not become a whole person. For her part, the female learns to give up her identity, suppress her initiative, and become passive. She is not a whole person, either. As a result, society functions in an extremely unbalanced and fragmented way. Another aspect of this distortion, particularly in the case of the female, is that she is often abused, treated as chattel, or even deprived of full citizenship rights such as the right to vote or the right to own property. As a result, many women hate being female.

In modern culture, as an antidote to the traditional passive female role, it has become acceptable for women to imitate men, becoming aggressive and competitive in order to be respected participants in the economic system. This is not a remedy to the imbalance between the sexes. The aggressive, competitive masculinity they are emulating is a distortion of true masculine qualities, such as initiative, courage, discernment, and decisive action tempered with love.

When women try to behave like caricatures of men, they minimize their unique feminine qualities of intuition, inspiration, and receptivity, and devalue their roles as nurturers and carriers of the culture—all of which could help save the planet. When men adopt distorted feminine qualities, becoming increasingly passive, dependent, and weak, they are not providing a solution, either. Consequently, the whole society is in disarray.

As a general rule, though, most people in this society lack, or do not express, authentic feminine qualities, while masculine traits are overemphasized to everyone's detriment. *In fact, the entire world is suffering from insufficient feminine energy, as evidenced by the terrible way we are abusing the planet.*

Spiritual Life Is Androgynous

Spiritually advanced people are naturally somewhat androgynous and have achieved an integration of the masculine and the feminine sides. A spiritually strong woman has access to dominant masculine energy that enables her to take decisive action, while a spiritually evolved man can easily express feminine traits such as humility and sensitivity. As we progress spiritually, we become more surrendered to the Lord, so that we are not controlled by what others think. When this happens, we are not so bound to traditional gender roles and can more easily express qualities attributed to the opposite sex. We are able to live spontaneously and truthfully without fear or false sentimentality.

We cannot go back home to God incomplete. This means we cannot go back home thinking that we are just male or just female. In order to progress, we must gain an understanding of androgyny, which is not merely physical or sexual. As mentioned earlier, society wants us to think that love is sex, and that in order to have relationships we must express ourselves sexually. However, remember that no one is more attractive than a highly evolved, spiritual woman or man. Everyone wants to be with such a person; that is natural. But this does not mean that the relationship must be overtly sexual.

When we start to unfold spiritually, we must monitor ourselves carefully to avoid causing disturbance to others. For example, as a man becomes more of a whole being, his feminine side will start to emerge. In this initial phase, such a man can feel so nourished by feminine energies that he wants desperately to experience them more intensely. Without vigilance, he may be attracted to one woman after another, feeling a need to be intimately involved with each. If he does not realize that this feeling is a result of his awakening feminine side, he can become promiscuous. A woman can have a similar experience, being drawn to a series of men as her masculine side awakens. If we are not careful, we can find ourselves engaging in indiscriminate sexual activity. We can see this phenomenon, for example, in some new-age organizations, in which men and women routinely practice "free love."

We must resist the urge to engage in unrestricted sexual expression. Ultimately we will just frustrate ourselves and others. This frustration can even become a factor contributing to a gay or lesbian lifestyle. Many women become tired of engaging in affairs, lamenting, "When I tried to find a man in college, it didn't work out. I tried to find a man at the office; that didn't work out. I tried to connect with an older man; it didn't work, and when I found a younger man, that didn't work, either. Then I tried to find a spiritual person, and still I got exploited. I've had enough. Now I want a woman." In the process of trying to find a mate, many women have experienced constant abuse, misuse, and exploitation, to the point that they have lost interest in men. But, unfortunately, a woman in this situation may continue to experience a lack of integration, because she cannot be fully whole if she is playing the dominant male role herself, suppressing her femininity.

Men can find themselves in similar situations, concluding, "Enough with these women. Let me find a man, someone who has similar experiences. At least we'll be able to understand each other." In some circumstances, such a man may simply lack strong masculine characteristics, easily becoming attached to another male who has dominant traits. He is actually seeking the man who is lacking in himself by trying to find it in someone else.

In today's society, many gay people may be the first to become deeply spiritual, because they have experienced frustration on all sides and are ready for a real change. They want a genuine connection with something higher. Their behavior is a cry for love, but since such a cry is not generally aligned to the developmental needs of the whole being, it can eventually lead to disturbance and confusion.

Resolving Differences

Men and women who want to live harmoniously together must not be afraid of conflict. This statement may seem paradoxical, but conflicts and differences of opinion are integral parts of any relationship. The beauty is that when love is mutual, partners can resolve the issues together. Even if we believe that we are not at fault, we can ask our partner, "How can I change? What can I do? What do you think would be the most spiritual way to address this?" A mate who cares will not suggest something impossible, and we will grow closer to the other person because of the exchange.

Your spouse might say, "You know, you really made a fool of yourself. You really shouldn't have behaved like that." At this point, you have a choice. You can say, "I was not a fool!

You're just envious. And what about you last week? You were worse." Or you can say instead, "What would make you happier about this? Let's talk about it." Then you can agree on a course of action to remedy the problem. If the first solution does not work, then you may agree to try something else. And even if you continue to disagree, at least your own willingness to talk can serve as an example to your spouse about how to behave in such circumstances. These situations are not so difficult if we have a sense of humility and are ready to grow and learn.

We often feel affection for those who reinforce our illusions about ourselves. By the same token, we generally have no time for people who refuse to support our faulty self-concepts. The more someone agrees with us, the better we feel, because this allows us to perpetuate our belief that everything is in order. Because we do not make corrections, our illusions increase, and the cycle continues. The ultimate outcome is confusion and unhappy relationships, because we are not willing to grow.

Sometimes we believe that our partner does not reciprocate our love. We are really admitting that we are in love with our idea of how the other person should behave. If our love is genuine, though, we will want to know of any problems we are causing and explore ways to remedy them. When we hear suggestions, we can ask for help in working on them. So where is the argument? Why do people make themselves suffer and create so much pain in relationships? It is completely unnecessary.

No relationship is without its problems. Sometimes the most wonderful relationships are also the most conflict-ridden. The only fundamental difference between a successful marriage and an unsuccessful one is the way in which the couple deals with the problems that arise. It all depends on our choices. We have to decide whether we want to suffer or whether we would prefer to make ourselves and others happy about life. We have it within our power to create healthy, positive relationships.

We cannot let someone else's behavior cause us to forget God and abandon our spiritual practice. It is more important to be humble and truly respect others. If our partner is anxious, then let us discover how we can help. Maybe we are responsible for the problem. As long as we believe we are right, or that the other person has to meet our demands, there is no possibility of genuine resolution. Nobody will be happy in such a house.

Offering Everything Back to the Lord

When we understand that God has given our partner to us, we ask ourselves, "Is God happy with the way I am treating His daughter or son?" Such an approach gives us more strength to tolerate difficulties in a relationship. When a problem arises, we may think reflexively, "That was an insult! I'm angry." But if we remember that we are caretaking for the Lord, we can move beyond our disturbance, interpreting the perceived insult as a cry for love rather than as an attack.

As we offer everything back to the Lord, we discover many keys to make our relationships work. If we are unwilling to look for these keys, all the seminars and workshops in the world will not help. Theories are meaningless if we do not live from the heart. Book learning does not work if we do not seek a deeper understanding of the individual, the human condition, and eternal spiritual truths.

Problems in a relationship are wonderful opportunities to discover our level of caring for another person. Such situations can test our willingness to be committed, honest, responsible, and accountable. Unfortunately, when challenges arise, one of the pair may start looking for an escape route, and the partnership gets shaken. But when we "hang in" and resolve difficult issues with our partner, the love increases because we have remained true to each other and cooperatively triumphed over adversity.

God-centeredness is essential in a relationship. When we think we are the proprietors, we cling to our money and other possessions. But when we understand that we are servants of the Lord, we realize that everything we have is actually a vehicle to allow us to offer our love back to God. This realization encourages us to become extremely loving and attentive, because we know that we are caretakers on behalf of the Supreme.

A relationship is an arrangement made by God to give us the opportunity to reciprocate His love for us. As we care for a husband, wife or, children, we gain the motivation to offer them the best of ourselves, even beyond what is necessary, because they belong to God. Our children are not ours alone; they are children of God. Our mate is not our property either, but is a representative of the Lord.

Are We Really Selfless?

When we act selfishly, we are feeding our own desires instead of serving someone else. We must examine our relationships carefully to discover where we are really directing our energies. Are we concerned about another person's welfare? Are we interested in that individual beyond superficial appearances? Is our focus spiritual? Or are we just intoxicated with our own importance, seeking first and foremost to feel good about ourselves?

What is most important in a loving relationship is the

quality of our caretaking on behalf of the Lord, not the benefits we gain. Whenever we view ourselves as caretakers, we dedicate our actions to the Supreme Lord. We are concerned, yet we do not see the other person merely as an extension of ourselves. We make every effort to give that particular soul the best we have to offer.

Of course, our best includes fulfilling our material responsibilities, but that is only the beginning. We must also give the other person what really matters, which is love, understanding, and spirituality. We should lovingly offer support and encouragement to our spouse, and raise our children to be God conscious, teaching them that they belong to God.

For this reason, a marriage requires a strong spiritual foundation. A marriage based on self-centeredness, economic security, or social convenience will very likely bring unhappiness. Such factors are transitory. The economic or social situations may change, the partners' attitudes may evolve, and all the reasons for forming the union in the first place may suddenly evaporate. When those elements are no longer important, nothing is left.

Attachment and Detachment

Attachment and detachment, important elements of spiritual life, are essential in marriage. But we must be attached and detached in the proper way, avoiding the extremes of being too clinging and demanding or too distant and indifferent. The question is: Exactly what are we attached to? Are we eager to give back to the Lord what belongs to Him in the first place, or are we clinging to our own desires for sense gratification? Our attachment should lie in offering everything to the Lord, whether it is our family, house, work, or possessions.

The fact of the matter is that we do not own anything, because everything belongs to the Lord. So, even if we try to become detached from our spouse and children, what are we actually giving up? If we claim to be detached, we are implying that we are now relinquishing something that we once possessed. This is a false conception. In addition, we should not use spiritual detachment as an excuse to become indifferent to those close to us. That is not loving behavior. Our duty is to employ everything to please the Lord without ever believing that we are the proprietors.

When we act as caretakers instead of proprietors, we try to please the Lord in our interactions with those close to us, because we understand that everyone is a representative of God. If parents did not feed their children properly, provide proper education, or take proper care of their health, the Lord would be displeased. Although our physical bodies are mere vehicles, still they belong to God, and we are responsible for keeping them fit so that they do not interfere with the functioning of the mind, intelligence, and soul.

Looking for a Mate

Although almost everyone wants a mate, many people have difficulty finding a suitable one. People looking for a marriage partner should be extremely clear about their priorities in life. When we go shopping, we usually know what we want. If we do not know, we wander aimlessly from store to store, buying a few random items and going home unfulfilled. The situation is similar when choosing a spouse. If we just wander from person to person, with no idea of the qualities we want, we may eventually wind up with someone completely inappropriate. At best, we will waste a lot of energy and become frustrated.

Once we decide what we want, we should put our needs on the table and look for someone who meets those needs. A relationship is a partnership, a matter of teamwork in which both people complement each other while working toward a common goal. Before making a commitment, a couple should examine goals together to discover whether they are on the same track. Failure to do so can cause serious problems.

We must understand the spiritual aspect of relationships. Men and women in committed relationships can help each other grow spiritually. If we have a mate, we should advance with our partner, or make sure that our partner advances with us. If we are growing and our partner is not, we will ultimately have serious problems.

A man and woman who are unclear about their priorities generally form a dysfunctional relationship. Both persons end up experimenting on each other, hoping to find an answer for themselves. When the experiment does not succeed, they discard each other in favor of new partners. In other circumstances, people without sufficient self-love enter into relationships hoping to find the love they want. However, as we have seen, two incomplete people using a relationship to make themselves feel complete usually cannot attain success. Each person is waiting for the other to make a miracle happen, and both parties wind up feeling cheated. Or it is like two thieves coming together to steal from each other. They will both cheat and get cheated, or they will both rob and get robbed. Obviously there will be no deep love or genuine peace in such a relationship. Such people will be failures in the school of love.

Once we develop a clear understanding of what is most important to us, we must not deny our needs just to find a partner. If we do, we will become more frustrated later on. We should be natural, allowing our priorities to speak for themselves and discussing them honestly with any potential mate. If the other person is not ready to accept them, then no meaningful relationship is possible. It is unwise to hope that another person will change. Those who cling to this idea are asking for misery. No fulfillment is likely for a husband whose wife becomes angry every time he engages in spiritual practice, or vice versa.

Let us not torture ourselves unnecessarily; we have enough difficulties already. We should seek a partner who allows us to express love in action, to enjoy life on a higher level, and to share our realizations with others. *We should not allow loneliness to drive us into an alliance with someone unable to share the most important aspects of our lives.* Eventually we will feel even greater pain than the original loneliness, because our partner will not be willing to receive what we have to offer. When we finally realize the futility of our efforts, we may have invested so much that the separation is wrenching. People can carry deep wounds from such experiences for the rest of their lives and never open their hearts to anyone again.

Seventeen Practices for Attaining Success in the School of Love

To develop meaningful relationships with members of the opposite sex, we must become whole human beings who have no need to look outside ourselves for solutions. Instead, we must learn to turn within ourselves and connect with higher, spiritual realities. How do we make such connections? The following seventeen points and practices, which summarize much of our discussion so far, offer guidelines for attaining the wholeness that can serve as a foundation for a strong, enduring relationship with a partner.

1. *Love is necessary for good physical and spiritual health.* Someone who is not part of a loving relationship is ten times more likely to experience chronic disease, and five times more likely to have a mental breakdown.

2. *Love is not a business arrangement or a contract with an escape clause for difficult circumstances.* We should not have this attitude or mood with our partner and surely not with God. We cannot approach the Lord in a mood of bargaining, and we should not begin our meditations and prayers with a long shopping list. Prayers of this nature are not based on unmotivated, unconditional love and do not help us develop the higher consciousness necessary to make us whole.

We do not have to remind God of our needs. The more we accept the fact that our lives are always under God's control, the more we understand that true prayer means: "Thy will be done." When we can sincerely offer such a prayer, we are becoming more integrated beings.

3. *Love is a decision that we can personally make at any time and under any circumstance.* No one has the power to make someone else love him or her, but each person can always give away love.

4. *Love is learning to love our true selves.* Those who do not care for themselves cannot love others deeply. The first love affair we must consummate must be with ourselves. One aspect of self-love is to observe four basic principles: no drugs or intoxication, no gambling, no illicit sex, and no meat-eating. All these indulgences can weaken our basic constitution. The more we allow ourselves to live according to natural laws, the more surrendered we become to the will of God. If we lack

self-esteem, we are refusing to see ourselves as children of God and do not have sufficient love and devotion to share with anyone else.

5. *Love is about a quest for wholeness, and if necessary, having a partner to share one's wholeness with.* People who think that some other person will make them complete or people who are waiting for love to come their way will remain impoverished and waiting. The more we become loving and whole, the more we will draw similar connections from the universe.

6. *Love is not about two desperate people, who are only trying to find fulfillment for themselves, coming together to rob each other.* Two extremely needy, selfish people coming together cannot make each other happy. They are too busy trying to take and get something for themselves at the expense of the other.

7. *Love is a holy relationship in which partners come together to serve and reveal their weaknesses and strengths for betterment.* In an unholy relationship, everyone especially hides their weaknesses. Such people are normally interested in erotic love (lust) rather than responsible, selfless love.

8. *Love is really the energy and hunger of the soul. When we are asking for love, we are asking for a connection with the soul, which is part and parcel of God.* We should not expect love to descend on us like an attack of epilepsy. It must be rediscovered at every moment by transforming lust into love, thus connecting us with our own soul and the souls of others. We are all starving for true unconditional love.

9. *Love is seeing our partner as a gift from God. We must go beyond merely loving our neighbors as ourselves.* We should actually love others—especially our mates—even more than we love ourselves. When we love our partners that much,

we realize that they have been given to us as gifts from God and that we do not own them. We are merely caretakers on behalf of the Lord, and our responsibility is to fulfill the Lord's wishes concerning them. Any attempt to dominate them becomes distasteful. Instead, we should make efforts to bring out their higher qualities—a practice that will also bring out our own higher nature.

10. *Love is seeing our mate as a pathway through which we can return our love to God.* The love we receive from our mate actually comes from the Lord, and our job is to send it back. Others channel God's love to us, and we channel His love to others. The Lord is engaging us in play to see what we do with His love. We can reciprocate God's love by caring for our partner with great devotion, as if God Himself were present.

11. *Love is sharing your realizations with your mate, which will help raise their consciousness as well as your own.* Then your relationship will become one of growth and acceleration. If you and your partner are not growing together spiritually, there will eventually be a breakdown in the relationship. Sometimes we fear surrender in spiritual life, afraid of having to give up our identity or afraid of loosing our partner. But we should understand that surrender to the Supreme is an opportunity to regain our full identity. Without a spiritual dimension to our lives, we are not integrated and cannot experience deep love.

12. *Love is a relationship with your mate in which you visualize a triangle with points A, B, and C. You are point A, your partner is B, and the Lord is C—all of your activities are God-centered.* Make an agreement with your partner to form this triangle as a permanent bond between you, so that whenever you meditate, chant, or pray, you are in connection with your partner and with the Lord. You do not necessarily have to meditate together or think about the connection simultane-

ously. Your agreement will work anytime and anyplace. In this way, you always keep God in the center of the relationship in all reflections and activities.

13. *Love is always viewing ourselves as love in action and carrying love wherever we go.* We want to be so filled with love that it naturally overflows to everyone we meet. In this frame of mind, we serve as representatives of the Divine in every aspect of our lives, consequently functioning as vigilant spiritual warriors.

We can practice love in action through the breath. As we inhale, we visualize ourselves absorbing the pain and frustration of our loved ones; as we exhale, we send happiness, joy, love, and peace back to them. Actually, this is not just a practice to help those close to us, but also the entire world. We inhale: we are concerned. We are not oblivious to other people's problems. We want to help. We exhale: we are breathing out love, compassion, and healing. This is not just an idle exercise. It has a powerful impact, and if we monitor the process over time, we will witness the beneficial effects on others.

14. *Love is about developing competitive, selfless relationships.* At first, this may sound strange and contradictory. How can we talk about cooperation, sharing, and selflessness, and then advocate competition? But actually no contradiction exists. In a spiritual context, competition means that we strive to be more selfless than our partner, seeing who can give more. We compete in reminding our mate about the Supreme and encouraging that person to move faster toward the Lord. The purpose of the competition is to assist one another in spiritual growth.

This process is only for people who want to be spiritual, who seek higher experiences beyond the flickering pleasures of material life. Such a competition in selflessness encourages partners to remember why they are in this body—

to become once again loving entities devoted to the Lord.

15. *Love is about offering the same quality of love you feel for your mate to everyone—but without the sexual component.* In other words, extend to others the love you have for the most lovable being in your life. We may wonder how to subtract the sexual element. Just remember that sex and love are not necessarily synonymous. Our love for our children can be extremely intense without any sexual overtones. No matter what the circumstances, try to develop that same kind of love in each of your relationships.

We all know the sweetness of loving just one person. Can you imagine how much sweeter it would be to have those feelings for everyone? Think of the loving exchanges that could develop, the reciprocation that would enrich our own lives and the lives of others. Unimaginable happiness, joy, and satisfaction would be our daily quota. We would no longer rely on particular individuals to give us this experience, because we would understand that we are really seeking God. The more we understand that God is in each person, the more we experience the Divine, and the more the Divine will make us whole.

16. *Love is having or looking for a partner to heal the world—not to escape it.* Normally many people seek out a partner to escape the world. They are miserable with life, and they feel that everything else can be tolerated or fixed if they somehow or other find that special person. We cannot heal the world if we are too wounded ourselves.

17. *Love is about treating all relationships as practice in preparation for the ultimate divine relationships in the Kingdom of God.* We should see all of our relationships as God sending us a partner to fix whatever has to be fixed before we join up with Him eternally. This means that we should practice seeing our mate as an agent of God, recognizing our own

divine nature, and remembering that we are children of God for whom great realizations and pleasures are available. Only in the Kingdom of God will we find the love and the eternal relationships we long for so deeply.

Ultimately, the real relationships and associations reside in their perfected states in the Kingdom of God. Right now, we are living in a school of unfoldment or love to help us become qualified to experience love far beyond anything that we can currently imagine. To do so, we must put God at the center. The Lord is in the heart of everyone, available to guide us. But we cannot go back home if we believe that we are just physical beings looking for happiness with the opposite or same sex. We can go back when we accept that we are children of God who have a chance to be with our loving Mother-Father God in an eternal realm. That is our natural birthright.

We take a step closer to that eternal kingdom each time we view a situation as an expression of God's divinity, or each time we act as another's caretaker instead of an abuser or exploiter. Remember, when we live in such a high state of consciousness, we encounter divinity everywhere until finally we begin to experience the realms of the spiritual world even while in the mortal body! The beauty is that we are always deeply in love with God and all His parts and parcels. We have just temporarily run away from the Lord and our divine associates.

Questions and Answers

Question: When you mentioned self-love, you said that loving oneself meant no drugs, no gambling, no illicit sex, and no meat-eating. Would you please elaborate on the meat-eating part?

Answer: It is very simple. We all know that the body is greatly affected by what we eat. An animal lives for eating, sleeping, mating, and defending. There is nothing wrong with that, because animals do not seek self-realization. But someone who eats animal flesh takes on some of the animal's qualities, which can interfere with spiritual advancement. In addition, from a nutritional perspective, many experts know that meat is not particularly healthy. From a spiritual viewpoint, one primary concern is the violence involved in animal slaughter. Such violence has a collective karmic effect, creating a strong possibility for violence in human society. In general, cultures with a tradition of vegetarianism display much less aggressive violence.

If at all possible, we should encourage our mate to adopt a vegetarian diet. We can make delicious vegetarian dishes to share. When we prepare the food in a loving state of consciousness and offer it to the Lord, the food becomes spiritualized and can be a powerful force for purification.

Question: If your mate just becomes more hostile and selfish whenever you try to be unselfish, what should you do?

Answer: If you have a partner like that, you do not really have a mate. A mate means a match, someone who complements you. If a man continues to exploit a woman who is trying to be more loving and concerned, she must realize that she is not in a functioning relationship. The more she tries to become spiritual, the more her mate acts to discourage her. She may have to find someone else, or it may be her *karma* in this lifetime not to have a physical mate.

Some people in this life may not be destined to have a partner. This does not have to be a major issue, because most of us do not remain in these physical bodies very long. And perhaps our partner, our real soul mate, is waiting for us in another lifetime. Instead of lamenting the situation, we can use the time to do intense spiritual work and get ourselves ready for our next steps. As we become more balanced, we will experience greater love for a growing number of people anyway. Then we will find fulfillment from these genuine relationships.

Question: An attractive member of the opposite sex will always turn my head. How can I get beyond seeing someone as just a body?

Answer: If we play the body game, we are eventually going to be disappointed, because our partner's body is inevitably going to change. So is our own. If a relationship is based on appearances, then before long we will become disgusted because the youth of the physical body does not last.

People are always changing form, although we do not often realize it. For example, someone we love may have an accident and lose a limb. Or a loved one may start growing old. The person we were attracted to originally now looks completely different, with less hair and more fat. Actually, the individual has taken on a whole new body. Sometimes we may be tempted to think, "That's not the one who attracted me. That's a different person altogether."

If a relationship is just based on superficial appearances or on how sweetly, poetically, and glibly we speak to our partner to cover up our inner emptiness, there can be no deep, genuine connection. Love must be beyond physical attraction. Sometimes relationships are on such a bodily platform that as soon as there is no physical contact, conflict arises without the parties even knowing why. They just experience great tension and anxiety as soon as the touching game stops.

Unfortunately, one day our senses—and our lover's senses—are not going to be the same. What will become of our relationship if it is merely based on sexual stimulation? If the relationship becomes empty, do we decide that God does not exist any more? Do we conclude that God does not love us or that He has cheated us in some way, simply because we are no longer experiencing physical pleasure with our partner? Will we cry out and curse the Lord, or will we try to understand more deeply how the situation can be an expression of His love? The school of love is full of challenges and adventures—only the deep lovers graduate.

Chapter 7

Loving Our Neighbors

All around us we see the results of the industrial paradigm's focus upon commodities and money, and its worship of fame, power, and control. As a result, modern culture does not give human beings and other living creatures the respect they deserve. Our planet—itself a living being—suffers profoundly from a lack of love. As we have seen, we treat the Earth and other species of life with such disregard that all around us are appearing symptoms of serious illness: floods, famines, earthquakes, droughts, hurricanes, plagues, and countless other scourges. In addition, instead of relating to other humans with love, care, and compassion, we manipulate and exploit them in a vain search for self-gratification.

Loving relationships are the way to counteract this negativity. Our personal relationships are a microcosm of how we deal with each other on an organizational, national, and global level, and how we treat other forms of life and the Earth itself.

Healing our planet ultimately depends upon how we relate to one another in the simple interactions of daily life. By relating to others lovingly, each of us can make a positive difference in our immediate environment.

In society today, many people do not experience sufficient love in their families, schools, or places of work. Love that cannot find a healthy means of expression often emerges in various perverted forms. We have already noted the rising levels of child abuse, incest, and rape all around us, as well as many other social and environmental ills. Sexual crimes are distorted manifestations of a natural tendency to love that cannot express itself constructively. Whenever people reject their own divine nature, their thwarted loving energy becomes a destructive force in the world.

The Need for a Culture of Love

This planet will not be healthy until we gain a deeper understanding of the soul and the universal love we all share. As parts and parcels of God, we naturally belong to a culture of love, liberation, and constant celebration. When we extend this love and joy to others, we experience ever-deepening levels of God's love. The world sorely needs a deeper sense of community and a more mature understanding of personal happiness, both of which depend upon our willingness to raise individual and collective consciousness by sharing our love with others.

Consider the "community" of a tree. Although the leaves of a tree require water, we do not need to water each and every leaf individually. In fact, if we water only the leaves and neglect the roots, the tree will not survive very long. But if we water the roots, we distribute water throughout the entire tree, so that the tree thrives quite nicely.

Although we may consider ourselves self-sufficient, we are actually no more self-sufficient than the leaves of a tree. The "nourishment" we need is love, and by directing our love toward God, we "water our roots" and naturally distribute love throughout the entire community.

Loving Our Neighbors Goes beyond the Surface

Materialism is rooted in duality; it is relative and impermanent. The material aspects of things are not their inner reality, and the materialistic viewpoint focuses on the outer manifestations without paying attention to the invisible essence. We cannot have meaningful, deep relationships by dealing merely on the level of our outer coverings.

A materialistic focus automatically disqualifies us from experiencing a deep level of love. Remember, loving others unconditionally is not based on a material understanding of life, because ultimately all love emanates from the reservoir of love, which is God. If we exclude God from the picture, we are merely attracted to material commodities and phenomena; we cannot experience unconditional love.

As we grow spiritually, we will be constantly amazed at the amount of love we can experience and share. The spiritual world is filled with eternal, loving exchanges that do not end, deteriorate, or disappoint. Even minor competitions and arguments in such an environment merely serve to encourage more caring and sharing.

We have all known of mothers who would sacrifice anything for their children, teachers who would go to any length to help their students, or husbands totally dedicated to the welfare of their wives and families. These simple examples of selfless relationships in the material world offer us glimpses into the spiritual realm of genuine love. As we saw in the previous chapter, if conflicts arise in intimate relationships, instead of producing a rift, they can cause even stronger bonding between the parties. The individuals understand one another better, and this deeper understanding allows mutual caring and respect to grow.

Loving and Trusting Others

Genuine love remains constant despite adversity. Love gives us the courage to maintain our position—even an unpopular one—in any environment. This does not mean that we should be foolish or naive. To deny unpleasant realities is to express the opposite of love; true love is based on honesty and trust, not avoidance. To love our neighbors as ourselves means to love them deeply, as we ourselves would like to be loved. It also means to trust them. Honesty draws honesty to itself, and trust attracts trust. Without these qualities there is no love.

On a practical level, we may wonder how to love an apparently unlovable person or how to trust someone who has not earned our trust. We can approach such a person as we would a troublesome child. Parents normally do not adapt their conduct to that of the child. Instead, they help the child improve by modeling proper behavior and encouraging what is positive. After all, everyone has some good qualities. Parents know their children's boundaries and are realistic about what is dangerous for them. They offer experiences according to their children's level of maturity, encouraging them to grow and protecting them from demands that might be too taxing.

If we refuse to view others as enemies even if they try to

hurt us, we can love almost anyone. *We must always remember that our so-called enemies have a desperate need for love, which they are expressing as best they know how, albeit in negative ways.* As spiritual warriors, we always have a choice in these circumstances. We can respond with compassion, or we can view these troubled people as enemies who have our destruction in mind. In the latter case, we become destructive ourselves, because we are categorizing others as harmful agents. But if we can see them simply as misguided seekers of love, we can remain loving and communicate that love in non-threatening ways.

We cannot love those whom we do not trust. So how do we extend our love and trust to untrustworthy people? Naturally, we do not want to victimize ourselves or others by ignoring their negative behavior. We simply must be intelligent enough to know their limitations, supporting their positive characteristics and refusing to provide temptations they cannot resist.

For example, we would not leave treasured possessions within reach of a thief, but if we secure our valuables, we can trust a thief even in our own home. We can trust alcoholics not to drink if we remove alcohol from their surroundings. In other words, we trust others by understanding their boundaries, removing temptations, and communicating our love. If we are clever enough to have a realistic view of their weaknesses, we can nurture their strengths to the point that they can even overcome their negative behavior. This is how, in the proper frame of mind, we can trust virtually anyone.

Keeping Secrets

Another aspect of trust relates to the issue of secrets and

confidentiality. Indeed, our effectiveness as spiritual warriors committed to helping others is closely linked to how we handle secrets. In the course of everyday life, almost all of us have kept secrets, shared them, betrayed them, or used them to exclude others and demonstrate our so-called superiority.

But secrets have no role in spiritual consciousness, because they create barriers between people, interfere with our expression of love to others, and imply that we have something to hide. Secrets create "in-groups" and "out-groups," polarizing people into categories of friends and enemies and destroying trust. *In spiritual life, each of our actions must be an offering to God and His agents, so that everything we do, say, and seek becomes a means of glorifying God. In such a situation, what is the need for secrets?*

Healthy communities should not be overly attached to secrets. In fact, the lives of spiritual warriors should be open books, because the Lord is watching everything. The more God conscious we become, the more those around us will experience enlightenment, exhilaration, and love. Unfortunately, many of us still do not want to be fully accountable to God—or even to our peers—and so we resort to secrets. We do not want anyone else to know what we have done, out of fear of being condemned for our behavior.

Our unwillingness to be accountable implies that we can hide from the Lord. Of course, we cannot. Remember, the Lord in the heart witnesses everything we do. We should offer all our actions to the Lord with enthusiasm as part of a loving program of service for which we want to be accountable and recognized. When we think in this way about all our actions, we have nothing to hide, and we no longer desire to keep secrets.

Confidentiality

There is a difference between secrets and confidentiality. Certain actions are confidential, but not secret. For example, husbands and wives make love. That is part of their experience of exchange in conjugal life, and it is confidential—indeed, few aspects of life are more confidential than exchanges of love. Yet even when a husband and wife procreate, they do so in the conscious effort to glorify God. Their behavior becomes an offering and, although it is private, it is not kept secret.

Confidentiality is often necessary for the development of trust, which, as we have just discussed, is an important aspect of love. That is why we have confidential aspects to our lives. However, although we are keeping parts of our experience from public view, confidentiality does not imply an intention to exclude. Rather, we simply do not want to cause unnecessary disturbance and so, instead of revealing everything at first, we share information gradually.

Spiritual life requires confidentiality in situations where the entire truth would be dangerous to others. For example, in sixteenth-century Bengal, Lord Caitanya freely preached love of God to the public, but reserved certain intense spiritual experiences for a few highly evolved, prepared souls. Premature exposure to such experiences would be mind-boggling for the ordinary religious person. Lord Caitanya's intent was not to be exclusive, but rather to protect those who could not handle such a level of intense love. This is the proper use of confidentiality.

Parents who love their children behave in a similar fashion. As the children grow, the parents explain the same facts over and over again, each time with greater depth, according to the children's capacity to understand. At first, parents may simply tell very young children to stop a particular behavior. Later, they may state the moral and ethical reasons behind their command. Still later, they may teach the children in greater depth why such behavior is unacceptable.

In each instance, they are explaining the same behavior at different levels. Confidentiality in spiritual life functions in the same way. A teacher can explain certain spiritual principles on an introductory level to the general public, go into more depth with an initiated group of disciples, and explore the same topic even more profoundly with a group of advanced students.

For example, beginners in spiritual life first learn a few elementary truths, such as: we are not the body, we can have a personal relationship with God, and spiritual life is about intense levels of love. Because newcomers are not overwhelmed with too much information at the outset, they can hear these teachings without resistance. After the initial exposure, they can gradually gain deeper realizations according to their level of readiness. Confidentiality actually makes it easier to offer the higher knowledge when the time is right. Without it, new students might become overloaded and reject the entire body of teachings before ever having a chance to understand them.

The Value of Making Judgments

In addition to understanding the role of secrets and confidentiality in spiritual life, we must develop a proper understanding of judgment. The widespread resistance to judgment in our culture, particularly among "new age" groups, derives from the refusal to accept a universal standard against which to evaluate our actions. But this refusal does not mean that such a standard is unavailable, nor does it excuse us from being accountable.

Many people tend to equate spirituality with peace, tolerance, and acceptance. However, tolerance is not always divine and peace is not necessarily a sign of love. These qualities indicate a mood of serenity that does not always address the requirements of the situation. When we seek peace and tolerance, we may be trying to cope with, manage, or deny the existence of an improper situation. For example, are we truly loving if we tolerate a son's drug addiction? Certainly not. A parent who avoids judgment to keep the peace in such a situation is behaving irresponsibly.

Spiritual life is based on love, which means service to one another through deep involvement and intensive interaction. Such service includes judgment and evaluation. Being judgmental in this situation indicates that we care enough to be our brothers' and sisters' keepers. If we refuse to be judgmental, we are being irresponsible and uncaring. Proper judgment is an integral part of spiritual advancement, because constant evaluation is necessary for growth. In order to progress, we must evaluate ourselves and be open to assessment from others.

Absolute Criteria of Spiritual Life

When we follow a bona fide spiritual path, we learn to judge our progress according to authorized criteria. We make similar evaluations in everyday life. For example, art collectors judge paintings according to standards accepted in the art world. Musicians improve their performance by following certain specified techniques. Think about it. Can we tell a martial arts master not to be judgmental toward his students? Can we tell a potter not to be judgmental toward her apprentices? Can we tell a teacher not to be judgmental toward his students? If he gives everyone an "A," his pupils have no valid measure of their accomplishments.

These evaluations are not based on whims or feelings of the moment, but on objective standards. The external criteria prevent us from being fooled by our own distorted perceptions. In spiritual life, teachers, saints, and authentic scriptures help us judge correctly, protecting us from the delusions of the false ego, which can easily lead us astray. To avoid error, we must rely on authorities soundly based in an established spiritual tradition.

Laws Are Universal

Rules and regulations are facts of life, governing everything we do. If we park on the wrong side of the street, we get a ticket. If we do not pay our taxes, we are fined. If we are consistently late for work, we may lose our job. If we reject all forms of judgment, we are implying that laws and rules have no function in society.

However, laws are necessary to maintain civilization and order. Of course, some people are law-abiding and others are not. We do not discard all laws, though, just because certain individuals dislike or disobey them or because a few laws are unjust or uncomfortable. At the same time, to be effective, laws must not repress our energies or constrict us unnaturally. Instead, they should protect us, inspire creativity, and enhance our sense of well-being.

It is true that some people misuse judgment and hurt others in the process. This is not true judgment, however, but condemnation. When we judge, we should not project our own negativity onto others, nor should we have ulterior motives. We should never use judgment as an excuse to close our hearts to anyone. At the same time, if we wish to help others or make advancement ourselves, we must understand the necessity for proper judgment and evaluation.

To believe otherwise is to imply that we are fine the way we are, even though we are often full of nonsense, deviating from absolute spiritual authority and indulging in behavior that can cause serious problems for ourselves and others. To accept poor behavior is not a sign of love, but of denial. Love is about growing together and learning from our mistakes. We should demonstrate enough love to help each other make the necessary corrections.

Instead of telling people not to be judgmental, we should beg them to be just the opposite. If they truly love us, they will gently but firmly appraise our behavior and show us areas that need improvement. By the same token, we should do the same for them, viewing their negative actions as cries for love and seeking ways to help them if we can.

Therefore, it is our duty as spiritual warriors to help each other evolve. Often we are afraid of judgment from others simply because we do not want to face ourselves and make the necessary changes. We are still attached to our ingrained habits of sense gratification. But if we want to make spiritual progress, we must have the courage to pull these old, destructive habits up by the roots. Judgment is an invaluable tool in the process.

Evaluate Ourselves First

Many people who need help may be unwilling to accept suggestions at first because their egos get in the way. They cannot believe that they could have made a mistake so easily, or else they are afraid of change. Frequently, they will only learn from crises, calamities, and chaos—in other words, from the "school of hard knocks." That is a slow way to learn, but nonetheless it is extremely common. Does any of this sound familiar? This is not merely a pattern in those we are trying to help. We have all engaged in such behavior at one time or another.

In order to overcome the temptation to judge others harshly and unfairly, we must always evaluate ourselves first before evaluating others. Unfortunately, some people try to find fault with others as a way of avoiding the necessity to look within themselves. Their judgments carry little weight because they are not based on a loving desire to help. Instead of offering constructive feedback, these people are simply seeking scapegoats. In order to be helpful judges of others, we must be vigilant about our own weaknesses and constantly strive to improve.

We should always maintain a spirit of humility, never counseling or teaching others in the belief that we have nothing to learn ourselves. From my own experience, for example, each time I give a lecture, I focus on something I would like to understand better. Then even if everyone falls asleep, I am excited because at least I have learned something. Otherwise, teaching is like a performance in which we are merely trying to please the audience. Eventually we will get to the point of saying things we do not mean, and people will know the difference.

To evaluate yourselves more efficiently, we advise you to solicit feedback about yourself from those who know you well. Approach them with pen and notebook in hand. When you are listening to their responses, write them down without comment or reaction. Then review them carefully later. In this way you will be sure to remember the suggestions accurately, without the distortions and rationalizations caused by false ego, self-delusion, or wishful thinking. You will not be so tempted to justify yourself or to dismiss what others are saying.

Everyone wants to grow, and we are all being used to help each other. But sometimes we may not be receptive to what others have told us. In such cases, after writing down the feedback we can put it away for a while, until such time as we are prepared to address it. When we review the comments later, we will be surprised to see how the Lord is constantly giving us a chance to grow and purify ourselves. We will also be shocked to see how often we refuse His help. But if we begin to understand that everything in our lives happens for a reason, we will begin to appreciate how closely we are being guided and how much God loves us.

How to Remain Positive

When we do not trust others, or when we attack them harshly without looking at our own behavior first, we are hurting ourselves most of all. We are also harming those we love, closing ourselves off in a misguided attempt at self-protection. In either case, we are demonstrating that we ourselves are not sufficiently loving, because we are unwilling to view objectionable behavior as a call for help.

Spiritual warriors put no one out of their hearts. They love everyone, finding positive qualities in each individual even if such qualities are well hidden. *As spiritual warriors, then, we may recognize that some people are immature, but instead of condemning them, we should look for loving ways to protect and guide them.*

Difficult people are like antiques: they have potential beauty despite their rough spots. For example, if we love antiques, we may cherish an eighteenth-century chair enough to get it upholstered again and again. Because the piece is important to us, we find a way to make it functional and beautiful. Similarly, if we genuinely care about family, friends, and associates, we will make our relationships sweet, defusing difficult situations and helping those who engage in unproductive behavior to improve.

To categorize others in a negative way means that we have already decided they are inherently selfish, unloving, or untrustworthy. We cannot help them turn weaknesses into strengths. Instead, having assumed that their limitations are insurmountable, we have cast them in a mold from which it is almost impossible for them to escape. Rather than sharing our love, we have reinforced their shortcomings by relating to them according to our narrow definition.

No matter how positive we are, situations may arise in which people reject our love, advice, or support. How do we express ourselves in such circumstances? The wisest course of action is to remain firm and steady, without reacting negatively or giving up. We must not change who we are or alter the love we feel. If we react negatively to a person who refuses our help, something is wrong with our own consciousness. We are seeking self-gratification because we want to be viewed as magnanimous, wise, or powerful. Our love is conditional.

We do not have to manipulate others in order to receive their love and respect. We should live simply and authentically, uncontrolled by the opinions of those around us. If we are genuinely loving, people will be naturally drawn to us. The only requirement is that we express ourselves truthfully, accepting the fact that some people may like us and others may not.

Under no circumstances should we try to change just because someone does not approve of us.

Negative Behavior Is a Call for Love

As spiritual warriors seriously interested in uplifting the consciousness of this planet, we must always remember that everyone values love above anything else. *In all circumstances, a person's words and deeds are either exchanges of love or cries for love.* Although we can easily welcome and appreciate expressions of love from others, their cries for love can pose a challenge. These cries can take a variety of forms that may appear diametrically opposed to love. For example, how often do we perceive the need for love behind someone's anger, rudeness, jealousy, indifference, or cruelty? Our first impulse is often to strike back in self-defense or to return the behavior in kind, but this only succeeds in driving the wound deeper and reinforcing the other person's sense of inadequacy, deprivation, and separation.

Whenever we experience difficulty in a relationship, instead of taking the other's words and behavior at face value, we should probe beneath the surface, asking ourselves, "Where does this person feel a lack of love? How can I help?" When we view the situation as an expression of the other's pain or need, rather than as an attack or a deliberate unkindness, we may become more willing to transform any impulse to retaliate into a desire to be of service.

We can understand this universal search for love in all interactions by examining our own feelings in different circumstances. Suppose we become angry. We can easily see that anger originates in our experience of feeling unloved. The other person has thwarted our hopes and expectations of receiving attention, respect, kindness, care, or some more tangible token of love such as a particular gesture or gift. As a result, we feel deprived, undervalued, and powerless. Because this is an intolerable state of affairs for most of us, we become angry, substituting the power of our wrath for the pain of feeling unloved.

If we are envious, we feel an emptiness and inadequacy within ourselves. We are disturbed that another person is receiving the recognition, wealth, or happiness that we want and believe we deserve. This, too, is a longing for love, which would give us a feeling of wholeness and completeness that we are sorely lacking.

We could say the same for a wide variety of other negative emotions. Fear is a reaction to a situation in which we anticipate harm, attack, destruction, humiliation, or even death. We feel alone and vulnerable, separated from the love we so profoundly need to feel connected and safe. When we hate, we are striking back in retaliation for the love that did not come our way when we wanted it. When we are cruel, rude, unkind, or deliberately indifferent, even though we may be completely unaware of the true meaning of our behavior, we are sending out powerful distress signals indicating our desperate need for love.

As spiritual warriors, then, we must remember that each time we interact with another individual, we are either sharing our love or expressing our need for love. Others are behaving in exactly the same way. People who are unkind, demanding, hurtful, angry, or sad are actually crying out for love. We should always be conscious of this universal need for love and share our own generously. *In every situation we must ask ourselves, "What is the love factor here that I need to address?"*

Dealing with Negativity in Others

In all circumstances, it is our job as spiritual warriors to respond positively to the cries for love that underlie negative behavior. There are three important ways we can respond when someone attacks us:

- *The first is to examine ourselves to discover our own lack of sensitivity, skill, or caring.* If we scrutinize our motives and actions carefully and sincerely, we will almost always find some element that we have contributed to the problem. Then we can take corrective action in all humility.

- *The second aspect of our response is to remain centered and to radiate loving energy, while refusing to get involved in arguments.* Since we are unwilling to take the offered bait, our would-be opponent may back off. No one likes to feel ineffective. Aggressive people generally feel foolish if their negative behavior has no impact, and they stop it quickly. In contrast, if we react to someone's attack by attacking in turn, we will experience great tension and anxiety. The other person has already defeated us because we have agreed to abandon our higher principles to participate in a hurtful game. Such a reaction demonstrates that we still have much work to do on ourselves.

- *A third way to respond to an attack is to demonstrate to the aggressor how much we care.* Even if the individual rejects our efforts, we will feel better because the love and generosity we have offered become part of our own experience. Obviously, if we become angry and disturbed, we have not helped anyone, least of all ourselves. When we offer genuine love, not only are we calming the other person's disturbance, but we are also offering a remedy for the deficits that caused the upset in the first place.

When we respond calmly and lovingly without reacting, we prevent the other from causing harm and also serve as a role model, demonstrating alternative ways to function. Remember, spiritual warriors do not merely seek to protect themselves; they also want to elevate consciousness and offer help. Whenever they do so, they are improving the level of consciousness in the world.

If we are afraid of being exploited, we may have trouble responding constructively. Instead, we will simply expect others to treat us as we have treated them. Cheaters worry about being cheated, just as thieves fear becoming the victims of theft. In contrast, spiritual warriors draw love from their surroundings no matter where they are, reinforcing the positive vibrations that are already present and helping these to increase.

Dealing with Racism, Nationalism, and Genderism

A particularly widespread aspect of negative behavior in the world today takes the form of racism, nationalism, or sexism. Many members of modern society are filled with hatred toward those unlike themselves. As spiritual warriors, we must not react negatively to the disrespect and injustices perpetrated by prejudiced people. Remember, we cannot fight successfully on a battlefield if we are angry; we lose clarity and dexterity. Our anger, frustration, and despair can also cause serious disease or dysfunction in our own bodies. And finally, if we are filled with negative emotions, these feelings will spill over into our relationships, particularly with those we care about the most.

This does not mean that we should simply deny the existence of racial, nationalistic, or sexist behavior by trying to pretend that everything is in order. As human beings, we require some measure of self-protection. We must refuse to allow ourselves to be victimized by prejudice, remembering that if others see us in racial, nationalistic, or sexist ways, this reflects their own level of consciousness.

Even violently prejudiced people are children of God who have temporarily forgotten their true identity. We should feel sad for such persons, because by being inhumane to others they are destroying their own humanity. Our approach should be to love the person—the soul, which is their true essence—but not the actions. In this way, without condoning destructive behavior, we can remain true to our mission of serving others by being living demonstrations of love in action.

Developing Meaningful Service

Although spiritual warriors do not seek any material reward, many of us have not yet attained a sufficient level of selflessness to practice such altruism regularly. Some egotistical motivation is usually involved in our helping others. This is not all bad. If we help children in a day care center, assist battered women, or feed the hungry, we are engaged in constructive action. There is nothing inherently wrong with our desire for praise. This longing for recognition is simply a step along the path of learning to offer everything to God.

The problem, though, is that we cannot always count upon the outcome we want. Sometimes we may not get the credit we think we deserve, or our actions may upset others. If we base our willingness to help others on expectations of praise and recognition, we may abandon our efforts as soon as we stop receiving acknowledgment.

Whenever we find that we are attached to appreciation from others, we should not give up our activities. We should continue, making every attempt within our consciousness to offer the fruits of our labor to the Lord. After all, even if no one acknowledges our contributions, God knows about them. Our job is to offer the best we can regardless of the consequences.

Remember, too, that real consciousness-raising is not based on how well we plan and organize activities, although these functions provide an important supportive framework. At the core of our service, beyond any structure, must be a loving concern for others. Countless people have begun humanitarian or spiritual work with good intentions, only to become so caught up in bureaucracy that they forget their original purpose. They become attached to fame and distinction, or they become jaded, treating people like cogs in a machine. Their work no longer uplifts consciousness and so loses its ultimate value.

The more we help others selflessly, the more the Lord bestows blessings upon us, even if outwardly our efforts appear to be unsuccessful. Remember, as spiritual warriors, we are ultimately concerned with uplifting consciousness rather than with improving material well-being. We cannot measure the value of our work by the extent of our physical accomplishments. Instead, our success depends upon the amount of consciousness-raising that occurs because of our actions.

It is far better to affect one person deeply than to try to touch many people in a superficial way. The changes that occur in that one individual will have a greater impact on the collective consciousness of the planet than slight alterations in the lifestyle of scores of others. Sometimes the simplest actions can affect another person's level of consciousness—a warm embrace, a kind comment, or a loving smile. We can all make efforts to uplift others in these uncomplicated ways, no matter what our circumstances and regardless of our skill level.

The Goal Is to Become Transcendental

Our goal as spiritual warriors is to become transcendental. Often, people engaged in helping others do not understand what this means. Anything transcendental attacks the basic grain of the material universe and reaches beyond it. In contrast, traditional established religions often try to help people become more comfortable with material life so that they will experience less pain, anxiety, or frustration. Many are content with that level and remain there.

But transcendentalists are not satisfied with such aspirations and seek higher dimensions of experience. They express a love that is sufficiently strong and deep to serve as an inspiration to everyone and to prevent the negativity of others from penetrating their own consciousness. In other words, those who are transcendental experience life above and beyond the mundane activities of the everyday world. They remain loving even when the environment is not, and thereby uplift the general consciousness of the planet.

As we explained in Chapter 2, being transcendental does not necessarily mean being sweet and gentle, and it does not mean staying in a relationship no matter what. That is a misunderstanding. When we are transcendental, negative people will either change in response to us or feel sufficiently disturbed to leave us alone. In some cases, we may choose to keep ourselves away from them. We should always be ready to help, but if others consistently reject our assistance, we may eventually decide to go away, calm in the assurance that we have done our utmost to extend love.

Remaining in a hurtful situation is often an invitation to be exploited. It makes no sense to continue giving our time and energy to those who cannot, or will not, reciprocate. As long as they see that we do not object, they will continue their unacceptable behavior. The more we demonstrate our care and concern for such people, the more they think we are weak, and so will continue to take advantage of us.

If we tolerate such actions, we are reinforcing their error. To end the mistreatment, we may have to remove ourselves from the scene and love the person at a distance. This does not mean that we stop offering unconditional love. On the contrary, we are expressing our love. It is an act of love to prevent the other person from accumulating more negative *karma*, which we accomplish by making ourselves unavailable for misuse.

The Struggle with Illusion

Becoming transcendental is not easy. As we persist in our spiritual practices, great challenges and temptations will arise. That is how the material universe operates. As we grow spiritually, gradually escaping the domain of illusion, the material energy clings to us intensely and refuses to let us go without a fight. For this reason, we must keep the goal in mind as we progress along the spiritual path. When the way becomes difficult, our focus on the end result helps keep us moving forward.

We should never depend on our own strength and intelligence in our struggle with material illusion, because the material energy is stronger than any one of us. Instead, we must rely on the Lord, who resides as the Supersoul in the heart of every living being and offers all kinds of assistance when we make ourselves available. If no help seems forthcoming, it is because we lack the faith to understand how personally the Lord is monitoring and assisting us.

We are risking a fall whenever we try to use our own strength to master lust and temptation. It is just a matter of time before we experience a situation we cannot handle. But if we realize the constant danger and remain watchful, our attentiveness will keep us from falling into the grip of illusion. The problem arises when we fail to take temptation seriously and so relax our vigilance.

Spiritual people mainly fail for two reasons: money and sex. Lust for money causes many spiritual people to give up their integrity and, in the face of economic problems, misuse of money can become an enticement. In addition, as we have seen, the pervasiveness of lust in this society causes many people to misinterpret loving behavior as an invitation for sexual contact. Many lonely individuals will deny their higher understanding in order to gain any taste of love, even if merely on a physical level.

As we become conduits for loving energy, our relationships become more profound. We become less eager to manipulate others to satisfy our own appetites, because we have developed sufficient inner strength to understand who we are, what the soul is, and how we relate to God. We no longer seek ultimate fulfillment in the material world.

Questions and Answers

Question: My son thinks I criticize him too much. Is there a difference between being critical and being judgmental?

Answer: It is a matter of consciousness. If your son is not taking care of himself, or not being serious about his studies, you should be a stickler. It is your responsibility to monitor his well-being, even though he may prefer to play eighteen hours a day. Your role is to assist and encourage him, and in order for you to fulfill this role properly, some evaluation is necessary. But even as you try to help your son, you must also respect his individuality and independence. Be careful not to make him an extension of yourself. Talking down to a child, even though your intentions are good, may provoke resistance and resentment.

Sometimes when you share something with him, he may perceive you as critical and dismiss your feedback. Yet if you see a need, you must be eager to offer yourself no matter how he responds. If he resists or feels attacked, then you can try to fill the same need in a more palatable way. Parents must always be vigilant and yet not so overbearing that they psychologically hurt their children.

Parents have the responsibility to protect, monitor, teach, and guide; that is all. If you notice that your son is not dressed properly, out of concern for his well-being you tell him to change his pants. You are not critical, just practical. You may want him to be careful when he rides his bicycle. You are doing your part to guarantee his safety, but you are not attacking him or blaming him.

He may not always appreciate your monitoring, but as a concerned parent, you must always be ready to give him your love, support, and guidance. Offering our feedback is part of our responsibility as parents. Indeed, a parent who does not intervene when necessary either does not care or is too afraid of what the child may think.

Question: I am someone who does not trust other people. In my case, it is really a learned behavior based on past experience. How do I deal with that?

Answer: As we discussed earlier, you should not be naive, foolish, or in denial. Instead, you must see things as they are. You may have learned from past experience that someone is a chronic liar or a thief, but you must not allow this to interfere with your present growth and development. Instead, when you are with that person, you should simply be careful not to present any temptations that could be too difficult. You would not give a sharp knife to a little boy. This does not in any way disturb your love, compassion, and concern for him. In fact, it is because of your love that you remove the potential source of harm from his environment.

Make an effort to see each person as a part of God. Then even if someone attacks you, you can look upon the experience as the Lord's arrangement for your growth. Remember, there are no accidents in the universe. Your attacker is really a divine agent of God—one who is temporarily in a state of bewilderment or amnesia—sent to point something out to you. Your loving perception of your would-be adversary can uplift that person's consciousness. The individual may even change completely, apologizing, smiling, and asking for forgiveness. On the other hand, if you meet an attack with a counterattack, communication becomes much more difficult. You both go away disturbed.

We are really talking about deeper faith. When you have deep faith in God, you start noticing that God appears in your life in many different forms and circumstances. Your job is to be ready to love and experience God in whatever way He presents Himself. He is trying to increase your awareness by making you more sensitive to your own impurities as you perceive the problems of others. In other words, the Lord is showing you what to work on in yourself by creating situations that expose your shortcomings.

What is the price of a life of fear and mistrust? You pay dearly in terms of your own love, compassion, and concern. You shut the doors and windows tight, keeping harm away, but allow nothing positive to enter, either. Although you should not be a fool, we would encourage you to open yourself up to higher levels of experience and love.

Question: Given what you have said about judgment, how are we supposed to interpret the biblical passage, "Judge not lest you be judged?"

Answer: If judgment and rules were not necessary, then God would not have given so many laws to the prophets. Such teachings tell us, for example, that adultery, fornication, blasphemy, and murder are sinful. Evaluation is necessary to help us recognize these and other sins.

However, we must judge with love and humility. The biblical passage you quoted is a way of reminding us not to concentrate on the faults of others when we are so sinful ourselves. If we criticize the shortcomings in others to avoid our own failings, we are not motivated by love. We are simply trying to hurt others in order to feel better about ourselves.

Judgment is present throughout the Bible. Much of the Old

Testament addresses the deviations of the children of Israel and the various attempts to set them straight. In the New Testament, too, filled with teachings of love and compassion, Jesus still throws the money-changers out of the temple, judging them fiercely. He offers parables, exhortations, and instructions to help people live more in accordance with God's laws. So the Bible and all great religious scriptures show us that evaluation, when motivated by love, is healthy and necessary.

Chapter 8

The Practice of Compassion

In today's world, we are surrounded by environments so hostile to our human and spiritual growth that higher truths cannot easily penetrate our consciousness. Yet these truths are just what we need. Physical reality is simply an external manifestation of something already set into motion at a deeper level, and material solutions to our problems will not work because they do not probe beneath the surface. To make lasting changes, we must make a concerted effort to look beyond the superficial aspects of any situation.

In all circumstances, regardless of any other remedies we may try, today's intractable problems call for deep compassion. Compassion sees profoundly into the heart of each situation and offers unconditional love as a remedy. As we gain more consciousness of our innermost spiritual nature, we understand that compassion can help us transcend the temporary and the relative aspects of things. Profound compassion is one of the most important spiritual technologies one must imbibe in order to be fully successful in life's school of love. This growing awareness can eventually guide us out of our negative circumstances. *As we open ourselves to compassion, our consciousness becomes more transcendental, and we radiate higher energies that uplift others and offer healing in a world of pain and suffering.*

A Prerequisite for Returning Home

The ultimate purpose of spiritual life is to go back home to the Kingdom of God, or the spiritual world. The practice of compassion is an essential aspect of our preparation for this goal. Preparation is necessary even in mundane life; it helps us function appropriately in various environments. For example, if we are going to a formal party, we prepare ourselves by dressing formally. If we are giving a musical performance, we rehearse thoroughly before appearing on stage. If we are in a play, we must learn our lines. Without proper preparation, we leave ourselves open to extreme embarrassment.

Similarly, we must be well prepared for our eventual arrival in the spiritual world. As we saw in Chapter 3, all the major scriptures emphasize that we are eternal beings who have a home far beyond the mundane realm of our material existence. We are out of place in this material realm, which serves as a training ground for higher experiences but is not where we can be truly happy.

Right now, we must prepare ourselves as expediently as possible to regain what we have lost and to receive the treasures that are awaiting us in the spiritual kingdom. No one can expect to enter the Kingdom of God without deep compassion.

Almost all orthodox scriptures—including the Bible, the Koran, and the Torah—instruct us to love our neighbors as ourselves. But loving our neighbors as ourselves, for all its value, can sometimes turn into a business proposition, because it is based upon the idea of exchanging one quantity of love for another. In such a situation, the love may be conditional rather than freely given. This is not transcendental.

As explained in Chapter 2, as spiritual warriors we must go further, loving others even more than ourselves. *If we love our neighbors even beyond the way we love ourselves, thinking only about the other person's welfare, we have become agents of compassion, and we are well on our way to becoming transcendental.*

When we selflessly align ourselves with transcendental consciousness, the universe will supply us with amazing support. Since we are no longer controlled by the normal limitations of the earthly realm, we can accomplish miracles. As we develop higher perception and higher love, we become so worthy to receive such blessings that eventually we will be "paroled" from the restrictions of the material prison atmosphere.

Beyond the Salvationist Mentality

Although compassion is a requirement for returning home to the Lord, we should not view it egocentrically as a means to enhance our own chances of salvation. Indeed, compassion extends far beyond any selfish motivation—even beyond the desire to enter into the Kingdom of God. For this reason, if we simply study a few techniques of *yoga*, seek to gain some psychic powers, or try to improve our own chances of being saved, we are engaging in elementary spiritual activities. In the final analysis, these are merely ways to cope with the prison environment and find some relief from the anxiety and stress of material life. They do not transcend this world of selfishness and so have very little to do with genuine spiritual realization. We cannot go back to the spiritual world with such a mentality.

Considering that self-centeredness interferes with spiritual advancement, we must constantly take inventory of ourselves and examine our thought patterns to root out selfishness. Most of the time we are preoccupied with our wants—not even our needs. We have become so accustomed to pursuing our desires that we distract ourselves from the experience of deeper love and happiness and from any steady feeling of well-being. Instead, we remain focused on the problems inherent in a world of duality, constantly feeding the senses and reinforcing the feeling of "I" and "my" instead of moving beyond them to higher pleasures. Even such a lofty desire as the wish for salvation is rooted in selfishness. Actually, salvation is something that happens automatically as we abandon our selfish desires and deepen our compassion.

The Meaning of Compassion

Compassion is unfettered by material restraints. The term "material" implies survival of the fittest, based on who is more dominant, controlling, and capable of manipulating others. Compassion is the opposite. It is a spiritual trait, based on selflessness and freedom from envy or any sense of proprietorship. It is not sentimental and it does not come and go with our feelings. When we are compassionate, we offer unmotivated, unconditional love to others, freely making sacrifices on their behalf.

Compassion is spontaneous and has nothing to do with guilt, fear, or resentment. If we offer help to others when we do not really want to, we are not motivated by compassion. In such cases, we feel compelled to act by the circumstances, offering ourselves grudgingly only because we have not found a way to escape. But the situation is entirely different when we give assistance to others in an exhilarated, joyful state of consciousness. That is true compassion.

If we profess to love God, we must also love His parts and parcels—all the living beings around us. A true devotee of the Lord is only interested in being a servant of others, viewing everyone as a manifestation of the Lord's energies. We can exclude no one from the range of our love and compassion, because when we serve others, we are actually serving the Lord.

Material life is full of countless misfortunes. If we are concerned only about our own comfort, or even our own liberation, we are clinging to a selfish orientation and cannot attain the ultimate goal of loving association with the Lord in His kingdom. But if we develop a deep level of selflessness and compassion, we become genuine servants who can share divine love with everyone regardless of their circumstances. As we encounter those who are suffering—the blind, the handicapped, the ill, the homeless, the imprisoned, the abused, or those forced to flee their homes, for example—we love them so much that we want to take their burdens on ourselves to free them from their pain.

Compassion Is Not Condescending

As mentioned earlier, we should all seek to become expressions of love in action, looking for every chance to serve.

However, we should be careful about our mood of service. Sometimes people have a way of parading their own supposedly evolved position by offering help with a condescending attitude that implies, "You can't cope, but look at how well I can handle this situation." We should never simply tolerate others or feel pity from a self-professed superior vantage point. Compassion is not about approaching others with the mentality of, "I'm going to be kind to you," or "I'm going to show you how good I am." Such attitudes are nonsense, and are the opposite of compassion.

Our attitude should be, "I am your Godbrother; I am your Godsister. I am your loving associate and I see that you are wounded. It is my desire and my duty to assist you." As we discussed in the previous chapter, we should view the other person's difficulty as a call for help—a call for our love, compassion, and service. Nobody wants to experience pain, confusion, or anxiety. *Even people who seem attached to confusion simply want attention—in other words, they want love.*

When we evaluate each situation from this deeper perspective, we can more easily remain undisturbed by another's hostile or inconsiderate behavior. We can say to ourselves, "Oh, this person needs love, and the Lord is giving me a chance to do some service. Let me see how I can help." When we think in this way, we are less tempted to merely tolerate the other person's weaknesses.

If we help other people without feeling compassion, they will only benefit superficially. Communication between people occurs more powerfully on the subtle than on the gross level. The feelings that we hold back are the ones that we communicate the most strongly. Therefore, the other person realizes, even if subconsciously, that we are just trying to demonstrate our superior wisdom and self-control. The recipient of our assistance will not feel uplifted because the help is not genuine.

Although this nonverbal communication of feelings can work in a negative way, as just described, it can also serve a positive function. If we act out of a genuine desire to help, share, and grow, then even if someone's ego tries to blot out our good intentions, on some level the message will get through. At a later time, if not immediately, the person will be able to respond.

Compassion Requires Courage

Compassion goes beyond ideas of "I" and "mine" and transcends notions of material comfort and security. When we practice compassion, we have no interest in power of any kind, not even psychic or mystic power. Forgetful of ourselves, indifferent to personal loss or gain, we feel the suffering of others so deeply within our own hearts that we dedicate ourselves to doing something about it. This requires great courage.

The innumerable problems in the world today require powerful spiritual soldiers who can move through heavy levels of contamination without being affected. Such warriors can help people who feel alone, abandoned, helpless, or hopeless—who go to bed in misery or who wake up in fear—to know that God loves them and that there is hope.

Those with Physical Challenges

Have you ever imagined what it might be like to be blind? Life for the blind can be extremely difficult. Because so much of what we do requires sight, they are often forced to depend on others who can see for assistance. When they are especially desperate for help, people may ignore them or even abuse them. If we want to become transcendental and develop qualities that lead us back to God, we must experience compassion for such persons. We must be willing to make sacrifices so that they can have a better situation in life, even if it means that we are renouncing our own security and comfort. Could we possibly see ourselves taking someone else's place to free that person from blindness?

What would it be like to have impaired speech? Visualize yourself unable to express yourself in words. Can you feel deeply the inner frustration that this situation would produce? How ready are you to take such a person's place? It is this level of selfless love that determines your readiness to return back home to the Kingdom of God.

We have all visited people confined to bed with a serious illness or unable to walk because they have become helpless invalids. Since they cannot take care of themselves, they have to depend on others to feed them, bathe them, and sometimes even take them to the toilet. Such dependence can be very humbling. In some situations, so-called friends and family members resent these persons, considering them to be heavy burdens because of their need for constant monitoring and assistance.

Frequently these persons create such difficulties that even their close relatives feel a sense of relief when they die. Family members may be just waiting, hoping that death will come very soon to remove their obligations. Is your compassion for these souls so strong that you would be ready to exchange places to free them from their torment?

The Homeless

Homelessness is a problem throughout the United States and around the world. Even in Washington, D.C.—the nation's capital—many people are huddled on the sidewalks, on grates, or in doorways, at all times of the year and in all extremes of weather. At the end of the day, these people have no family to console them, no refuge. As a contrast, think of your own life: In the morning you leave your comfortable home for your job or other activities, and at the end of the day you come back to spend the evening with your family or those close to you. Loved ones give us a purpose in life, infusing us with enough strength to go back out again the next day to meet new challenges.

But imagine those who have no work, no home, and no family. When such people finally find a place to rest on the street, children may stone them or the police may arrest them. Whenever we pass them by, we may avert our gaze or at most offer them a quarter. Is our compassion strong enough to allow us to feel their sadness and their misfortune?

Many people are so fearful, tense, and competitive these days that they revel in someone else's misery, feeling better when they find someone whose condition is worse than their own. If a calamity befalls a friend, they may offer words of sympathy and encouragement, but in their inner consciousness they are glad to have escaped such a fate themselves. Such an attitude is indicative of material consciousness. When our compassion is so strong that we are ready to take a homeless woman's place to free her from her torment, then we will be eligible for entry into the spiritual world—not before.

Those in Confinement

It is a sad commentary on American society that many citizens have become lawbreakers instead of leading a natural life. Modern society is not meeting the needs of many people. Our high rates of criminal activity and incarceration indicate that something is seriously wrong with society itself. In the United States, the most distressing part of the situation is that teenagers are committing so many crimes. Youth represent the future of any nation, but growing numbers of young people feel so angry, disturbed, and frustrated that they strike out at their environment in unproductive ways—some of them extremely serious.

Can you imagine being sentenced to life imprisonment without possibility of parole? Each day you wake up with nothing to look forward to. You may have lost all contact with the outside world, and even your own family no longer communicates with you. You wish that you had never been born, and your greatest anticipation is the moment of your death. You may want to commit suicide, but you do not have even this expression of freedom, because everything that could be used in such an attempt has been taken away.

To deepen our compassion and develop a sense of gratitude, we might want to break our normal routine and visit a prison to understand the plight of the incarcerated. Or we might choose to visit a hospital or a mental institution to remind ourselves how many people are bedridden, ill, and hurting. When we witness the levels of impairment and hopelessness that others suffer, we can gain a deeper appreciation of our own good fortune and make a firmer commitment to use what we have to help others. Once we have done so, we will take less for granted and understand that our complaints are often self-indulgent, occurring simply because our normal means of sense gratification are not available.

In Western society, our problems are rarely life-threatening. We can easily get caught up in our own personal frustrations and anxieties, complaining constantly and forgetting that millions of people are in circumstances far worse than anything we have ever encountered. We may complain that we cannot make our car payment this month, but at least we have a car. We may bemoan our inability to pay our insurance premium on time, but at least we are insured. Although the American welfare system is falling apart, most countries in the world do not even have welfare systems. In many developing nations, a handicapped person without a job and without a family for support would have to beg or starve.

Yet we take our social safety nets and our material prosperity for granted. Instead of being grateful and thanking the Lord, or dedicating ourselves to helping those who have less, we often complain about what is lacking. But, remember, if we want to graduate from the school of love and enter the Kingdom of God, we must be ready to make any sacrifice to ultimately help glorify the Lord and allow others to come closer to Him.

The Plight of Refugees

Think now of a refugee family, its members living like wild animals in primitive conditions, desperately roaming from one environment to another in search of food, shelter, and security. We have all heard news stories about the tremendous suffering that occurs when massive numbers of people are driven from their homes with no food, shelter, or medical attention. They are literally living from hour to hour.

We have no experience to compare to theirs. We may live from paycheck to paycheck, but they live from one minute to the next, wandering from city to city or from refugee camp to refugee camp, unable to relieve their misery. They are often profoundly traumatized, experiencing terror, pain, and grief from the violence they have endured in the past, suffering intensely in the present, and perceiving nothing but more pain, or even death, in the future. They may have been forced to run for their lives from the horrors of war, leaving behind all their possessions, while those most dear to them were killed in the strife. Their loved ones may have even been tortured and murdered before their very eyes.

Such refugees have to live with these terrible memories constantly, possessing nothing secure to depend upon and leaving behind everything that would normally serve as a foundation for a future. Because they have lost everyone and everything most dear to them, many may no longer have the desire to live. In effect, they have lost a large part of their identity.

How would you feel in such a situation? Everything that gave your life meaning has vanished. Those you love the most are lost, maimed, or dead, and you have to pick up the pieces of your life. You have nothing left; yet your ability to go on requires faith in a world that has inflicted tremendous pain and confusion upon you. Millions of people are in such a condition today, with little future to look forward to. The problem is growing even larger as racial, tribal, ethnic, and religious conflicts proliferate around the globe. In such circumstances the common people suffer the most—especially the children.

Although refugees may appear to be better off than prisoners, because they are apparently free to go anywhere they choose, actually they are just as trapped. And the children who have lived through such terror may be affected for the rest of their lives, never trusting anyone again. They may cry themselves to sleep at night out of grief and loneliness, and have horrible recurring nightmares because they have seen their mothers, fathers, aunts, uncles, grandmothers, and grandfathers murdered in front of them.

The Abused

Now imagine a small, helpless boy or girl being repeatedly abused by those who are supposed to be his or her protectors. How painful to contemplate an innocent child turning to his or her parents for love and care and receiving nothing but more torture! Child abuse is on the rise in our society. Abused children learn early to mistrust adults and to see the entire world as a hostile place. Millions of children have this perspective because they have experienced nothing but anger and violence.

Another growing area of abuse is that of the elderly. Imagine an elderly lady who has given her life to her family, only to experience isolation and humiliation in her old age. Her own children reject her and treat her with contempt. They forget that they too will become old someday, dependent upon others—perhaps their own children—who will supposedly love them out of gratitude and respect.

Sometimes this elderly lady's children beat her, knowing that she will not dare to fight back or tell anyone else. These ungrateful children become disturbed by the mere fact that she is still around. Like vultures, they take her money and other assets while she is still alive, hoping she will die soon so that they can collect her insurance and be finished with her once and for all.

How Compassionate Are We?

Do these situations move us to tears? Would we be willing to remain on this hellish planet eternally, giving up all concern for our own liberation, so that these souls could be free? Only if we can answer honestly in the affirmative will we be eligible for entrance into the Kingdom of God. Of course, the Lord will not actually allow any of His beloved servants to suffer eternally on behalf of others, but a high-level servant of God must demonstrate a genuine willingness to do so. The Lord becomes extremely attentive to those who have surrendered at that level of consciousness. Indeed, such a degree of compassion actually purchases the Lord's help to alleviate the hurt and despair of others.

Many spiritual traditions tell us that saints literally feel the pain of all those around them. Because they feel this despair so intensely, they are very careful not to give anyone cause for suffering. Instead, they rejoice when they can help someone else experience happiness.

Imagine yourself in any of the difficult or painful situations described in this chapter. Feel the intensity of suffering involved, and meditate on the type of love required to help souls who are hurting so much. As we have seen, deep compassion means that we are willing to take suffering upon ourselves so that others can lead better lives. We are not talking about mere religion here, but about a profound level of spirituality that requires great commitment. It is not for the faint-hearted. As spiritual warriors, we must develop a high degree of spiritual maturity to make such enormous sacrifices willingly and help raise the level of consciousness on this planet.

Such total commitment and intensity are prerequisites for entering into the environment of divine love. Spiritual life is not an extracurricular affair, nor is it merely concerned with providing us our "daily bread." Those who attain entry into the Lord's kingdom have moved far beyond concerns of guilt or fear of punishment, and they have no interest in what God can do for them. Rather, they understand that spiritual life is about making a change in consciousness so that they can totally offer themselves in service to the Lord and His creation.

At times, the extreme selfishness and intense suffering around us can be so overwhelming that we wonder if anyone is capable of expressing selfless compassion and unconditional love. Fortunately, though, there are always divine messengers who can teach us about compassion, providing role models that can raise our consciousness to a higher level of spiritual expression. Those who encounter such selfless beings are blessed with a rare opportunity to witness evolved souls in action who gladly forgo all personal gain to enable others to return back home to Godhead. Given the total commitment and infinite compassion of such saintly souls, how can we not be moved to emulate them? With their protection and assistance, we can accomplish miracles.

Compassion Is Spiritually Empowering

We attain deeper levels of spirituality according to the extent of our love and compassion. When we experience an intense wish to make dramatic changes for the better, we become highly empowered. Although the fulfillment of such a strong desire may be far beyond our own capacities, remember that our sincerity and dedication can attract the Lord's energies, enabling us to perform feats that we could never accomplish alone.

Many great prophets have had such empowering experiences. Some have arrived directly from the higher abodes as ambassadors whose mission is to make a serious difference on this planet. Still others, born on this Earth, have become so compassionate and intense in their wish to help that they receive divine empowerment. They feel the pain of others to such an extent that the Lord allows His divine energy to enter them and assist in their compassionate mission. In Vedic terminology, such an empowered being is called a *saktyavesa-avatara*.

Acting as agents for the Lord, they receive one of the greatest blessings that anyone in this state of evolution can experience: the ability to eradicate the negative karmic patterns of others, as Jesus did when he died for humanity's sins. The lives of such compassionate beings counteract much of the negativity and collective *karma* in society, giving people more opportunity to learn about the higher truths.

Help for the Disillusioned

The world's materialism constantly captures the senses and force-feeds us artificial nourishment that does not satisfy or sustain us. In fact, materialism acts as a slow poison. Something is seriously wrong when many of our most brilliant minds dedicate themselves to perfecting the ability to kill, or when one of the planet's greatest businesses is the illicit drug trade. A culture is not healthy when it stockpiles enough chemical and nuclear weapons to annihilate everyone on the planet many times over.

As we saw in the first chapter, the impotence of our spiritual leaders prevents them from counteracting the widespread negativity in today's world. Consequently, everyone is increasingly subject to demonic energies. In such an insane world, we should avoid trying to fit a warped mold and we should not be afraid to be different. To adapt to such a crazy environment is a sign of real insanity, and to be different can be a healthy, thoughtful position.

As spiritual warriors, though, we must understand the prevalent atmosphere and not be surprised when people reject our help. They may be caught in the thrall of sense gratification or feel powerless to fight against the behavior all around them. In addition, they may have been disappointed in the past and are afraid of being cheated again by spiritual messengers. They hold themselves back as a means of self-protection.

Yet compassion requires us to act. If we are too cowardly to share our love and devotion unabashedly with others, or if we are too afraid of being singled out for our so-called eccentricities, we are part of the craziness and will be of little help. Although we must not force ourselves on anyone, as our love and compassion become deeper and stronger, we will surround others with such a powerful spiritual radiance that they may begin to accept us and what we have to offer. When we remain equipoised, fixed, and consistent, disillusioned people may begin to realize that our behavior is not based on any ulterior motive. Because people really desire the best for themselves, once they are convinced that we genuinely want to help them grow and advance spiritually, they will become more open.

Insufficient Love Is the Problem

We must always remember that most of the world's suffering is not because of material conditions, but because of insufficient love. Think of the rage and aggressiveness of many children today. Given the environment in which they are being raised, it is almost impossible for them to behave otherwise. As products of self-centered and exploitive unions, they have been conceived in violence, with no expression of genuine love. In the womb, these children hear only anxiety, frustration, anger, gloom, and despair. After they take birth, they are exposed to the same atmosphere. At every critical developmental stage—indeed at almost every moment—life treats them with hostility, abuse, and neglect. These souls have never met anyone who really cares about them.

Sometimes, though, certain people from these environments escape the usual fate. They do not turn to drugs or crime, and they are not in prison. Instead, they become politicians, doctors, social workers, or educators with genuine concern for others. How do they escape the hostility and degradation of their surroundings? When we look at their backgrounds, we discover that at least one person in their lives made a difference. Someone truly cared about them, and that person's love transformed their consciousness. They gained a sense of motivation and self-respect that gave them the strength to resist the negativity around them.

We never know when we are playing an important role in the life of another soul. We all affect each other in subtle as well as obvious ways, and sometimes we are unaware of the impact we have on someone else. In these times when so many people are suffocating from the heavy impurities of the planet, a little breath of fresh air, a little opening, can make a huge difference—especially if it is potent. We cannot emphasize enough the importance of our small, seemingly insignificant gestures. The more we manifest the divinity within us and express it through compassion, the more we can uplift those we meet in the course of daily life.

Becoming Receptive to Higher Energies

As we contemplate the problems in society and feel a desire to make a difference, we must develop our inner resources in order to be capable of offering service. We cannot give what we ourselves do not possess. In order to have something valuable to share, we must purify ourselves and live in a more transcendental way. Then our interactions with others will be genuine, emerging from our inner core rather than being superficial behavior adopted for the sake of appearances.

The effect we have on others is based on who we are and the energies we radiate. On the physical level, we may not have to do much to make a difference. As we interact with individuals and their environments, our own love, devotion, and higher awareness are automatically communicated to others, who in turn can also make an important difference.

For this reason, we must work on ourselves so that we can naturally radiate love and compassion. Such work is not at all egocentric. We become like soldiers preparing to go into battle. Any interaction with another person abounds with subtle influences and exchanges that are far more penetrating than external appearances might suggest. Once again, the little words, simple expressions, and kind gestures that we share with people in need are often much more beneficial to them than the dollars we put into their hands.

Spiritual practices such as reading, meditating, or chanting can help prepare us for greater service to humanity and the planet. However, our motivation for such practices must never be to enhance our material situation or to gain psychic or spiritual leverage over others. We should always ask ourselves, "How can I develop and grow so that I can share?" That kind of attitude, accompanied by humility and compassion, can make us more receptive to higher energies.

The Art of Self-renewal

If we want to serve others effectively and with steady compassion, we must also learn the art of replenishing ourselves. Leaders, as discussed in Chapter 1, are not the only ones who require rest and renewal to perform their functions properly. We all have a similar need for self-care as we fulfill our daily responsibilities. Some members of the helping professions—social workers, nurses, or doctors, for example—can become extremely jaded and insensitive because they try to help others without taking time for themselves. Eventually they become caught up in the lower energies of the people they are dealing with, which causes them to be callous and unkind.

We can renew ourselves by prayer, meditation, diet, or by taking time away from the environment and exposing ourselves to an influx of spiritual energy to cleanse our consciousness. Chanting or *mantra* repetition can be a tremendous help. Many traditions use beads as a support for chanting or *mantra* meditation. When spiritual practitioners chant on these beads, they are praying, "Dear Lord, somehow I have fallen away from you. Please pick me up. Please allow me to be of service once again." The chanting also allows people to cast off many of the negative energies that surround them constantly at work or in the streets.

Imagine what it would be like to see people's thoughts as we go through the routines of our daily lives! Visualize yourself in a city, commuting home from work on a bus. Now imagine that another passenger is angry. The impact of that anger is the same as if the person were throwing a rock at you. Another person is fearful; somebody is disturbed; and yet another individual is envious of what you are wearing. You are actually sitting on a bus with fifteen or so people bombarding you with rocks. Is it any wonder that you walk away wounded? Your physical body may not feel it, but your subtle body has been attacked. You carry all those bruises home with you.

Chanting, or repetition of a sacred *mantra*, allows us to heal those wounds. It builds up our resistance so that we can ward off these onslaughts against our consciousness. That is why so many traditions emphasize the importance of calling on the names of God. Even in mundane life, when we call someone's name, we are inviting that person to notice us and come to us. In the same way, when we speak the Lord's name, we are summoning His presence. Chanting the holy names can be a powerful practice that invokes the loving protection of the Supreme Personality of Godhead. It can also be a most important way to help us become profoundly compassionate.

Questions and Answers

Question: What happens when people reach such a level of selfless love that they are genuinely willing to take the place of those who are suffering? Can they actually do so, and what happens to them?

Answer: People with a strong level of compassion and selfless love are ready to make sacrifices to allow others to excel, even if it means they have to share their credits or give them up altogether. When there is no other way to assist, they can share their strength, love, and spiritual energy to help someone else. God will intervene on behalf of someone who really lives and thinks this way.

The problem is that normally we try to control, manipulate, and dominate others. Consequently, we keep experiencing all kinds of miseries. Remember, spiritual realization is not something imposed on us or a state of being that we can get from outside. It is something dormant within us. Our outside experiences are meant to help us develop more faith and gain more clarity about how to access the realization we already possess. We have simply covered it over with innumerable superfluous concerns. In our insanity, we try to run away from those states of consciousness that are most beneficial for us.

Question: My mother has an aging dementia, which is like Alzheimer's. It keeps getting worse, but she has no physical deterioration. I have just assumed that this situation was her *karma*. Am I wrong? A friend recently asked me why I don't help her more.

Answer: We should always try to heal ourselves and others. Some people are active healers and have the ability to channel healing energy or allow the Lord to use them to help someone else. But we are all healers, because we can always help others raise their level of consciousness. Every sickness has a consciousness component, and we can help others learn to live better so as not to get sick, or to use the sickness as a means of acquiring more spiritual realizations. We can show those who are ill how to avoid being depressed and overwhelmed by the illness.

To be healers, we do not necessarily have to lay hands on someone, offer prayers at a distance, or engage in other types of metaphysical activities. We can simply assist others, by helping make improvements in their character or by helping to relieve them of some of their suffering, even if it is nothing more than just a visit and a few kind words. If we are carrying a higher, spiritual energy, we will automatically uplift the other person's spirits by our natural radiation.

As you speak to your mother or read to her from any of the scriptures, even though her mind may not understand, her soul will. As you allow yourself to connect with her in a spiritual way, she will be able to receive what you have to offer. Unfortunately, sometimes nurses and doctors unwittingly discourage, or even kill, people by the comments that they make when they think a patient cannot hear or understand. People who are anesthetized or in a coma can still take in what we say on some level.

Under anesthesia, although the body is asleep, a part of one's consciousness is still active and extremely receptive to the surroundings. Under such conditions, a negative comment about a patient's prognosis can be devastating, because the unconscious accepts it as the truth. Someone who has been exposed to such words may become depressed and hopeless for no apparent reason. That is why people in the caring professions should be careful to manifest higher energies and to speak positively, lovingly, and with compassion at all times. They can help their patients heal faster and more completely. On the other hand, if they are not careful, they can destroy any chances for recovery.

Question: Many spiritual organizations are talking about purchasing rural land to develop self-sufficiency and to get away from the dangerous, violent conditions in the cities. Is this compassionate? If we are all trying to save ourselves, how do we help those who need us the most?

Answer: First, understand that those persons and organizations that are leaving the city just to save themselves will be part of the devastation. This is not compassionate behavior. Everything that happens on this planet is highly monitored. People are aligned to various energies based on their consciousness. Those who are trying to get away from any environment just for reasons of self-preservation are already deeply caught up in egotistic nonsense, and they will carry the same nonsense wherever they go, because their consciousness has not changed.

That being said, urban life is unnatural. Factories, pollution, superficial commodities, sealed buildings—all this and much more is completely contrary to a natural way of life. In cities, people have little ability to grow anything. They must depend upon supermarket food, as well as upon electricity, elevators, gas-fueled cars and trains, and many other manufactured items that remove them from the natural order. Rural environments, where we can rely on nature to a greater degree, are healthier. In such an environment we can connect more easily with higher energies because there is less interference.

Although many people are fleeing the city just to save themselves, there are others who have an unselfish, compassionate motivation. These individuals and groups are trying to demonstrate to others how to become self-sufficient and live off the land. They are making efforts to implement the motto, "Simple living and high thinking." Such people and communities are in a more exalted position that brings divine protection.

Keep in mind that many souls may have to meet physical death as the Earth cleanses itself. This cleansing is concerned with consciousness, and many souls will have to be recycled. But many other souls will be able to remain here to help create a sort of heaven on Earth. In fact, a great number of souls have deliberately come to this planet at this time to finish up some work for their soul's evolution and so graduate to the higher realms. What happens will be based on each person's level of consciousness. God never leaves any of us alone at any time. Higher agents are always ready to help us.

There are particular environments, such as many rural areas, that attract evolved beings from the higher realms more than others. When we spend time in such environments, we can more easily become aware of the presence of these beings. That is why it is very important to develop some connections outside of the city. In rural settings, we are more likely to have a sense of control over our destiny and experience more natural ways of life. We can express more of our higher nature and consequently become more fit to help others. Such environments provide powerful support for the practice of compassion.

Chapter 9

Love of God

You will remember from Chapter 2 that the great Vedic scripture known as the *Srimad-Bhagavatam* describes an assembly of sages who were concerned about the highest truths and the spiritual welfare of humanity. When these wise men inquired about the most profound spiritual knowledge, they learned that the *yuga-dharma*, or the supreme spiritual activity for this age, is pure, unconditional love of and service to God. Such love is not dependent on externals or on various rituals, but is based on consciousness.

Longing for the Lord

We are all ultimately looking for a relationship with God. In our day-to-day activities, as well as in spiritual life, we are looking for a particular *rasa*, or "taste," of relationship. *Rasa* is different in various relationships. For example, the *rasa* between friends is different from the *rasa* between parents and children or the *rasa* between lovers. In the material world, such connections are a pale reflection of the deep, loving varieties of *rasa* we can have with the Lord. As we become more genuinely loving, accepting more of our divinity and connecting more with God, we can have powerful relationships, far exceeding anything we have ever known in this lifetime.

Our purpose as human beings is to fall back in love with Mother-Father God and return to the land of divine love, where we can experience our natural state. Anything else is unnatural. If we are not totally absorbed in divine love, we remain subject to the bondage of lust and the sufferings of old age, disease, and death—all part of the material environment and not in alignment with who we truly are.

We must ultimately understand that we exist completely for the Lord. When we have such an understanding, we love God totally with our entire being. Such a loving state does not erode our own identity; on the contrary, it expands it, increasing the depth of our experience as we offer our love to the Lord and then receive it back in reciprocation. Our expression of love brings more love.

We can never be fully satisfied until we are back in our natural state in the spiritual kingdom, where relationships are all God-centered. That is why a daily spiritual practice is so important. It prepares us for the intense love and service of the spiritual world. We should practice with complete dedication and devotion, far more intensely than if we were a violinist preparing for the most important concert of our lives.

When we love others, we suffer deeply if we do not see or hear from them. We desire to know everything about them; we yearn to speak with them confidentially, to spend time with them, and to receive letters from them if they are away. If we have all of these feelings here in the physical world, imagine how much more intense these longings are when they are directed toward the Lord.

If we make spirituality our top priority, we can make contact with the spiritual realm right here and now. *The truth is that God and His agents want to connect with us far more than we want to connect with Them.* When we sincerely put God first in everything we do—one hundred percent, not just partially, theoretically, or occasionally—we begin to experience what we have previously only read or heard about. The spiritual world becomes a part of our own reality.

Love of God Is Not a Demand

Although everyone wants to experience love, when problems arise we often become resentful and discouraged. The real test is to remain firm in our love of God no matter what. Otherwise we are simply viewing Him as a menial servant whose role is to fulfill our desires and whims. In such circumstances, we are like spoiled children, turning away or throwing tantrums if He does not give us what we want. Love of God must go beyond such an attitude.

Many of us do not understand the necessity for pain and suffering in our lives. "If there is a God," we ask, "why is there evil in the world?" If there is a God, why doesn't He give people—and me in particular—whatever is necessary to be happy? If suffering is a reality," we conclude, "God cannot exist." This outlook, based on self-centered desires for gratification, assumes that God should be responsive to our wishes at all times. It does not take into account our own misuse of free will and the karmic consequences of our actions, nor does it acknowledge the educational value of our experiences, including the difficult ones.

In literature, the tragic hero often learns through various types of adversity, eventually emerging a stronger person for the experience. The same process of growth is available to us through the Lord's infinite mercy. Indeed, if our bond with the Lord does not get stronger in times of adversity, then we are not operating from a platform of deep love.

Fear of God

Many people believe that fear of God is a prerequisite for spiritual life. A case in point is the reaction to an address made a few years ago by the president of Ghana (some say as a result of my influence) to an assembly of priests, entrepreneurs, and politicians. In his speech, he mentioned that instead of fearing God, he was learning to love God. The churches condemned him roundly for this pronouncement, saying, "What kind of man is this? How can he be our President? How can people vote for him—a man who does not fear God?" These religious leaders did not understand that a connection with the Lord can exist that is far deeper than fear.

Children who fear their parents and teachers only behave properly under a threat of punishment. If the external pressure is removed, these children will do anything and everything. It is the same in our relationship with the Lord. An affiliation with God based on fear cannot be very strong. It remains on a superficial level, preventing us from developing the deeper understandings necessary for true spiritual realization.

Fear prevents us from giving ourselves freely or developing

deep connections with others. Instead, we direct our primary focus to avoiding unpleasant consequences. Love, which is an expression of free will based upon appreciation and spontaneity, cannot thrive in such an environment. Unfortunately, many religious traditions operate on the basis of fear, worshiping a God who punishes violators of His laws. Followers of such traditions expend their energies more to avoid chastisement than to express love.

Yet fear can play a useful role in the early stages of development. When children are young, parents must resort to rewards and punishment. At this initial level of dealing with authority, children are self-centered and motivated mainly by fear. Later they begin to understand at a deeper level, saying, "I love Mommy and I don't want to do that because it will bother her," or "Daddy will be very unhappy if I do this, so I won't do it." As they mature, they learn to perform actions based on love. It is the same in our relationship with God. At first, we may fear Him—often a necessary step, because at least we recognize His existence. Eventually we develop a broader understanding, discovering that spiritual life is not merely a matter of rules and regulations, but of the soul's communion with the Divine.

Doubts about God

As long as we are in the material world, we will continue to have doubts about God. If we had no doubts at all, we would no longer be human, and would not require a material body or a material consciousness. We would already be residing in the spiritual kingdom.

We should not be concerned about our doubts. As we saw in Chapters 3 and 4, the mind and the senses like to be in charge. When the mind and senses discover that we are tuning in to transcendental energies, the mind, under the control of the senses, throws tantrums to draw our attention away from higher realms of experience. Eventually, though, we realize that the mind plays these "doubt games" in order to avoid being controlled or ignored. When we understand this, we will not take the mind's tricks so seriously.

Instead, we must strengthen our spiritual practice so that our intelligence, in contact with the soul, will direct the mind. Then our faith and understanding will be strong, and we can let the doubts just be. As our faith and understanding increase, the doubts will fall away—making room for new ones, of course! Eventually, though, the more we allow the soul to emerge, the less disturbing our doubts will become.

Although we must overcome our doubts, we must also remember that religion is not just a matter of blind faith. It is true that faith is necessary in everything that we do, materially as well as spiritually, but properly directed faith should turn into realization—in other words, into direct experience. Spiritual life is an exacting, sublime science, and we have certain keys to make that science work for us. Without leaving this body, we can make contact with the spiritual world. If our practice does not yield results, either we are not being expert in this practice or our faith is based on an improper belief system.

Levels of God-realization

People on various spiritual paths refer to the ultimate goal in different terms: *nirvana*, *samadhi*, cosmic consciousness, entering into the mind of God, or becoming one with God. Yet all these terms pertain to energies of the spiritual realm that emanate from the Lord; they do not refer to the Lord Himself. When we bake a cake, we can smell the fragrant aroma throughout the house without ever seeing the cake in the oven. As another example, although we have never visited the sun, we can experience its warmth and bask in its radiance. In the same way, without meeting the Lord face to face, many spiritual practitioners aspire to experience the divine energies of the Lord.

But this is only one aspect of spiritual life. As we study spirituality more deeply, we discover that there are different levels of God consciousness. As we said, the process of becoming God conscious is extremely scientific. At the level just described, that of experiencing the Lord's effulgence, we begin to feel a oneness with all creation and with the Lord's energies. Beyond this is another level of God consciousness in which we discover the Holy Spirit, or the Supersoul—the presence of God in our hearts. Yet higher is an experience of God in which we enter into the spiritual realm. Even here there are different levels and divisions, as Jesus indicated when he said, "In my Father's house there are many mansions."

We Need Deep Spiritual Experiences

Many of us are starving spiritually. Because we lack deep spiritual experiences, or because we do not have role models who have such experiences, we tend to become mechanical, dry, and faithless. As pleasure-seeking beings, if we do not experience pleasure from spiritual sources, we will eventually start filling the void with material activities.

Some people used to get disturbed that my spiritual mentor constantly repeated the same theme in his books and lectures: "You are not the body." They wanted him to address more confidential, esoteric subjects. He did not comply with their requests, though, because such matters are not meant for extensive discussion. They belong instead to the realm of inner experience.

If we use our intelligence and our mind to speak of experiences that actually belong in the soul's domain, we can become confused and distort the truth. Just as words cannot describe colors to a blind person, they cannot fully give us an understanding of the esoteric realm. That can only come from direct experience. In order to gain such understanding, we must work on our character, dissolve our impurities, and increase our devotion, so that eventually we become worthy of transcendental knowledge and bliss.

In spirituality, there is always a higher level to attain. No scripture by itself gives us sufficient information to reach the spiritual world. That is why teachers and spiritual guides are necessary. To avoid being misdirected, we must be sure that the messages of our teachers are aligned with the scriptures and with other realized practitioners of the path. When they are, we can feel comfortable with them as mentors. If we practice properly, we will gradually obtain the results described by the saints and scriptures, gaining windows into the spiritual world and becoming more eager to attain even higher experiences.

In order not to sidetrack our spiritual development, most elevated souls do not parade their mystic abilities. They realize that such demonstrations would attract people to their powers rather than to their devotion, and they do not want to encourage the belief that spiritual life is just a matter of certain tricks or techniques. Sometimes we think that seeing God is a matter of knowing a particular formula. We wonder, "How can I see God? How can I hear the universal sound? How can I have a guide?" As long as we persist in our belief that spirituality is a matter of technique, remaining unwilling to go more deeply into what we already have and resisting the need for self-examination and self-purification, we will stay on the surface of spirituality.

It is our state of consciousness that matters in spiritual life, not just external religious forms or practices. The language we use for prayer is not important, nor is where we pray—in a barn, a cathedral, a temple, or our bedroom. All the externals are details to help us attain greater inner experiences. If the internal spiritual connection does not develop, the externals become almost a waste of time.

But if we do not have role models to offer us proper reinforcement and coaching, we may settle for mediocrity. By so doing, we cheapen the scriptures and teachings of our path, because we imply that high spiritual attainments are not possible in our tradition. Such an attitude minimizes the genuine accomplishments of the many qualified spiritual teachers and practitioners who do exist and allows us to feel comfortable with a low level of attainment.

Look For the Inner Teachings

Every tradition has inner teachings. Each of us should try to learn more about this deeper knowledge in our own tradition, for it helps us see beyond the external aspects of religious life. The Lord's love and compassion are universal. Those who are caught up in external, exoteric practices tend to become sectarian, and sectarianism is responsible for many of the world's problems, setting one group against another and causing untold suffering. As we go more deeply into the inner teachings, we discover the common foundation of all spiritual traditions.

This is one reason why we should never read the scriptures as if they were merely sources of factual information or compilations of interesting myths and stories. We do not turn to scriptures just to get some data or to be entertained. The scriptures are as alive as we are; they are literary incarnations of God. For this reason, highly advanced souls can fall into a state of ecstatic trance after merely reading a passage. For them, the scriptures are not just words; they serve as connections to a whole realm of spiritual experience. When we read scriptures and other devotional literature with great love and care, we are looking through a spiritual window into the transcendental realm.

Certain teachings have existed on this Earth since the planet was created. Among these are the *Vedas*, some of the oldest scriptures known to humanity, which are based on realization and actual application of inner spiritual teachings. Even today, Vedic practitioners are available to transmit this knowledge to others in living, experiential form. These teachings can yield the same kind of results as they did in the past, provided we are willing to apply ourselves sincerely.

Love of God Is Intoxicating

Spiritual life is not about dry theories or constant struggle, strain, and self-denial. It is about profound experiences and exhilarating intoxication. Why should we cheat ourselves? We all want to love and be loved. We all want to experience the heights of pleasure. Ultimately, reduced to its simplest form, that is what spiritual life is about: the highest enjoyment, the greatest pleasure, and the most intense sense gratification—but far beyond the material level. We perform various austerities, rituals, and practices to prepare ourselves to transcend the shadows and images of this material world and attain the glories of the spiritual realm.

Remember that all living entities seek love, happiness, and pleasure, including people who behave in distorted or destructive ways. Can you imagine how intense your pleasure could be once all the barriers and limitations to its pure attainment were removed? We can gain a tiny glimpse of such a state when we experience a powerful, overwhelming feeling for someone we care about. So why should we hesitate to move closer to God and experience greater levels of pleasure?

When we begin to enter into higher states of consciousness, the physical body may not be able to contain the ecstatic experiences, which are literally beyond this material realm. Yet, although ecstasy is quite an intoxicating experience, it is only an initial aspect of the process of developing pure love of God. The feelings, symptoms, and experiences of pure love of God are actually far beyond this level.

As we grow spiritually, we develop a sweet competition with God, in which the more we try to serve the Lord, the more He is eager to bless and receive us. In such a situation, we feel such deep love for and reciprocation from the Lord that we believe He cares for no one but us. In this state of consciousness, we do not mind whether we are in heaven or in hell, because we know that we are loved. Every moment is an experience of giving ever greater love to the Divinity and receiving it back in overwhelming quantity.

The beauty of spiritual life is that we can attract divine grace from the Lord and, once we have received it, we can share that grace with others. If we encourage other people by offering our experiences and realizations, they may think, "I want to experience this, too. I want to be free of my miseries, or at least not be bothered by them. I want to have balance in my life and not feel torn in different directions." To lead a life on several different tracks is schizophrenic. We should not shatter ourselves like that, but instead integrate ourselves around these essential questions: How much do I love God? How much do I want His full grace and blessings?

Personal Association with God in the World's Traditions

God is more than energy, sound, or light. Just as there is form in this material world, God also has a form—but His form is spiritual. This makes sense if we think about it. There can be nothing outside of God, including form. So why would He not have a form? All forms of opulence, such as beauty, love, or knowledge, come from the Supreme Lord and are part of His totality. The only reason we can experience them at all is because they are part of the Lord to begin with.

Because the Lord has a form, love of God is not just an abstraction, but an expression of a direct, personal relationship. The advanced inner teachings of many traditions emphasize deep levels of love in the most personal way. Examine your Koran or Bible closely. You will discover many references to personal relationships with the Lord. These scriptures, as well as the Vedic writings, speak of seeing God face to face.

For example, a passage in the Hadith literature of Islam explains that the highest experience in Paradise is to have the vision of Allah. The Muslim scriptures also describe the Prophet's ascension, one of the peak experiences of his life. He was accompanied by the angel Gabriel from the lower to the higher planetary systems, until they reached a certain point beyond which the Prophet had to proceed alone to have a direct encounter with Allah.

In the Christian tradition also, God has a personal aspect. For example, the Beatitudes teach that the pure in heart shall see God. The Book of Revelations claims that those known as the children of God shall wear the sign of the Lord on their foreheads and see His face. In the scriptures of both Christianity and Islam, Sarah is described as treating God as if He were her beloved child. Abraham turned to God as to a friend. We cannot have formless energy as our child or as our friend. Parenthood and friendship imply a relationship based upon activities shared between distinctly different individuals, in this case one of them earthly and the other divine.

Spiritual Union

The world's inner traditions connect us with deep levels of personal experience. Sex exists in the spiritual world in the form of spiritual union, but we cannot understand it in our present conditioned state. *The physical sexuality of material life is merely a perverted reflection of the soul's eternal, pure, rapturous relationship with the Supreme Lord.* Although the reflection has certain attributes of the actual relationship, it is not the genuine article in its full reality. Sexual experience may seem pleasurable to us while we are in this conditioned state, but ultimately it does not give us the deep fulfillment we seek.

Yet we cannot simply categorize sex life in this material world as an illusion, believing that material life is unreal and that only spiritual life is real. Rather, the important distinction is that spiritual life is eternal and material life is temporary. Even an illusion is a reality in its own way: it is an actual phenomenon that takes on the appearance of something else. Although an illusion cannot stand on its own, we would be mistaken to deny its existence. For example, when we see an image of ourselves in the mirror, we understand that the image is a genuine two-dimensional reflection of a three-dimensional reality. The reflection has certain attributes of that reality, but it is missing many others. It is partial and imperfect. In the same way, the artificial, temporary experience of physical sex is an imperfect reflection of spiritual union. Although it does not give us what we ultimately want, it serves as a positive sign that the real, enduring experience of spiritual union does actually exist.

In the spiritual realm, union has nothing to do with physical bodies trying to stimulate each other, or genitals seeking pleasurable contact. Instead, spiritual union means that all aspects of the spiritual body unite with the beloved. As a matter of fact, in the Kingdom of God, the spiritual senses do not have the limitations that our physical senses do. For example, in our physical bodies we must use our eyes to see, because we cannot see with any other organs. Yet residents of the divine realm can see with every part of their spiritual bodies. The same is true for the other senses. One sense can perform the activities of all the others, because there is no differentiation among senses such as there is in the physical world.

It is because the physical body is limited and cannot experience any eternal, pure relationship with the Supreme that material sexuality can never fulfill the longings of the soul. Yet, even in this world, we can engage in sex life in a way that takes on a liberating aspect. In the *Bhagavad-gita* 7.11, Lord Krishna says, "I am sex life which is not contrary to religious principles." Physical sex has a valid role in spiritual life when we approach it as a service to the Lord—one that allows souls to take birth in this world to continue their journey back home to God. If we have such an attitude of service, we can engage in sexual activity without compounding our attachment to the material world.

In modern society, most people have sex on their minds every day. Although they may not know it, they are really desiring the most sublime experience of all—the highest connection of the soul in its rapture with the Divine Soul, the ultimate Source of all souls. *The problem is that those functioning on the bodily platform try to have union without union.* That is, they seek physical intimacy without knowing who or what they are. Believing themselves to be physical bodies, they consider the purpose of life to be merely personal gratification and stimulation. Unfortunately, their ignorance of the soul causes them to seek the experience of union through physical means. Because all genuine union is spiritual, their attempts can only lead to frustration and disappointment.

Confidential Aspects of Spirituality

Any attempt to understand spiritual sex, or spiritual union, must go beyond the formal, majestic, awe-inspiring conception of God as the Supreme Creator, Maintainer, and Destroyer. It must also leave behind the impersonal idea of God as light or energy. The deeper, more confidential aspects of spirituality involve an intimate, personal, rapturous relationship of the soul with God. When we are no longer bound to material consciousness and have no further desire for physical sense gratification, many types of intimate, sweet relationships with the Lord are possible. Such relationships form part of the inner teachings of any bona fide spiritual tradition, as experienced by the most advanced saints.

For example, the inner teachings of bridal mysticism in the Christian tradition include personal experiences with God, so that nuns in certain orders become brides of the Lord. In addition, the writings of St. Teresa of Avila and St. John of the Cross describe a mystical, conjugal, loving relationship with God in which the soul, feminine in nature, takes great joy in associating with the Beloved. In the ancient Vaisnava tradition in India, many of the great male *gosvamis* also write about being feminine in spiritual consciousness, considering themselves lovers of the Lord.

Unfortunately, in this day and age, people have become so external that they consider scriptural accounts of spiritual experiences as mere allegory or myth. Yet this is not the case. For example, the Song of Solomon in the Bible talks about a personal relationship with God as a lover. If we were to ask a minister to explain these passages, we might hear many kinds of conjecture. Yet, the poet of the Song of Solomon is describing an interpersonal experience in which he actually sees himself as a female and thinks of the Lord as a lover. The poem, which is not allegorical, but factual, describes confidential aspects of the soul's union with the Lord. It is a literal expression of a great saint's dedication, love, and ecstasy.

Loving exchanges in the spiritual world are not limited to these that occur face to face. Ultimately, expressions of love can be of two types: those that occur in the presence of the Beloved and those that occur when separated from Him. The love experienced in separation from the Lord is considered the deeper connection, because when the Beloved is not present the lover is completely absorbed in meditation on Him, anticipating the joys of reunion. This aspect of spiritual life demonstrates the great difference between physical sex life and spiritual union. Material sexuality relies largely on physical stimulation, whereas spiritual union considers the experience of separation to be even greater than the actual presence of the Beloved.

The natural activity of the soul is to be in constant rapturous union with the Beloved, or to be making arrangements for that union. This is another radical distinction from material sexual activity, which only occurs when humans feel the desire for it. In spiritual life, the soul is always experiencing blissful union, even more so when separated from the Beloved. Although this makes no sense materially speaking, it makes perfect spiritual sense, because union in the spiritual realm has nothing to do with physical bodies.

The difference between union in a spiritual body and sex in a material body is similar to the difference between water and oil. Although these are both liquids, if you drink oil you will die, whereas if you drink water, you will live, risking death only if you do not drink it. Another analogy is the difference between an altruistic, righteous citizen and a vicious, selfish convict. The citizen and the convict are subject to different laws and have different fields of activity. The prisoner's lifestyle and environment are perverted replicas of actual society. The convict's universe is the prison, while the citizen is free to go anywhere. Prisoners who forget about their incarceration and try to maintain their habits in prison without changing their criminal frame of mind can forfeit their parole. Similarly, if we persist in identifying with the physical senses in this material prison, we forfeit our ability to free ourselves from material energy.

The Realm of Eternal Romance

The highest level of the spiritual world is a realm of eternal romance centered around selfless loving exchanges in which we play the role of lover, parent, or friend to the Lord. The closer we come to a hot stove, the more warmth we feel. Similarly, the more we know about the transcendental realms, the closer we come to the Godhead. The greater our harmony with God, the stronger our contact with divine love. As we deepen our knowledge of the Lord's magnanimity, omnipotence, and omniscience—not just in theory, but in realization—we experience God's love in increasing measure.

An analogy may help clarify the nature of true loving connections in contrast to self-centered lustful associations. If we love someone deeply—a spouse, a child, a friend—we care about what happens to that person. We rejoice in the individual's successes and mourn the losses as if they were our own, and we want to help in any way we can. In spiritual union it is the same, yet at a higher level. The individual who serves another with love and dedication experiences as much, and often more, pleasure than the recipient of the action. For example, the Vedic tradition explains that the servants of Srimati Radharani, Lord Krishna's devoted consort, experience millions of times more enjoyment than even Krishna Himself. This is the nature of true loving relationships in contrast to self-centered, lustful behavior that merely seeks personal happiness, stimulation, and pleasure.

Imported into this material world from the higher dimensions, divine love is often beyond our understanding, because much of what we call love in this world is still based on egocentric concerns. We need help to experience it. Divine love reaches us through the agency of higher beings who come from the spiritual realms to teach, uplift, and guide us.

The humility of divine agents can be difficult to understand. An accomplished martial artist knows the power of his hands and feet. He can take a life in a matter of seconds. Because of this, he has a natural sense of humility, knowing the harm that can result from misuse of his skills. He also realizes that he will be held accountable for what he does. In the same way, divine messengers are aware of their great responsibility.

In the material sense, great power coupled with great humility may seem contradictory. A humble person is often considered docile—a wimp—and not powerful. But spiritually, these two qualities are quite compatible. Although the Lord's representatives wield enormous power, their humility is based upon great love for those who are in a state of amnesia, suffering unnecessarily lifetime after lifetime despite the availability of keys to end their unhappiness.

Spiritual messengers are humble for another reason: their performance is being monitored, and they will suffer the consequences if they do not execute their activities properly. Yet another cause for their humility derives from their dependence on the Lord. They recognize that He is the source of all power and love, not themselves.

Many bona fide teachers have the mission of aligning their followers with certain specific aspects of God's kingdom and not others. That is why teachers seem to differ from one another; they are summoning souls to experience different facets of love and service to God. Sometimes people will misunderstand this, believing that God has sent only one prophet or son. However, Jesus himself said that he could give people the power to become sons of God. If we follow any of the bona fide prophets with dedication and commitment, we can also become conscious sons and daughters of the Lord. Unfortunately, as we have seen, religions fail to understand this and fight each other to defend the exclusivity of their particular doctrines.

Go Deep Into Your Own Tradition

Problems arise when people do not remain faithful to their bona fide traditions, because they never go deeply enough into any teaching to gain meaningful spiritual understanding. But if they do stay true to a bona fide path, the scriptures and practices can open the door to God. If you feel most at ease with Catholicism, that is fine. This means that Catholicism is perhaps your way. If you like being a Muslim, then Islam may be your spiritual direction. Once you have made a choice, though, it is important to remain loyal to your scripture and practices, so that love of God can unfold in the proper sequence.

Paradoxically, we cannot respect other traditions without sufficient belief in our own. There can be no "interfaith" without faith. If people in different traditions do not have deep faith in their own scriptures, teachers, and practices, they will approach their own spirituality on a superficial level. Consequently, when dealing with other faiths, they will merely focus on the differences in external practices and be blind to the unity that exists beneath the surface.

What have people gained who wander from one path to another? Nothing more than frustration, a basement filled with books, and a bank account drained by all the checks they have written for conferences and workshops. They have not learned to give up their selfishness and body-conscious approach to life, nor have they developed any deep level of love and compassion. Instead, they have persisted in going outside themselves to find what actually resides inside.

Spiritual advancement requires love, commitment, and devotion if we are to gain the stability and understanding to go beyond sectarianism. When we have sufficient depth, we can appreciate any bona fide tradition. A deep experiential knowledge of our own teachings and practices allows us to respect others, at the same time remaining chaste and faithful to our own path.

Never forget this point: *We cannot serve the all-complete God in a myopic state of consciousness.* We must not be fragmented or partial. We cannot be limited and sectarian while claiming to be messengers of love. If we are genuine messengers of love, we remain loving at all times and in all places, sharing what we have with others. If we find ourselves unable to share willingly, then we have work to do on ourselves. It takes someone who is God-like to be able to connect with God.

How beautiful it is to hear people praying in other ways— what a wonderful orchestra! How rewarding it is when people of different faiths, races, genders, and nationalities work harmoniously together! If we think otherwise, we are accommodating the fragmentation that creates the world's most intractable problems in such places as Bosnia, Liberia, Rwanda, Burundi, Northern Ireland, or the Middle East. We must learn to align with people at a deeper level based on similarities in consciousness, rather than focusing on differences of dress, language, race, or religious practices.

Spiritual Life Is Our Rightful Claim

Spiritual life is our birthright and is accessible to each of us. To shed these material shackles, we must first realize what is available and then understand our responsibility to claim our rightful heritage. If we believe that the spiritual realm is beyond our competence to attain, or just too much trouble to seek, we are blocking our own progress. Spiritual consciousness is our natural state and is available to each of us if we genuinely want it.

When God becomes our first priority, we willingly do our part to purify ourselves and be of service. Then the mercy of the Lord's servants is always accessible, helping us conquer one obstacle after another and shed layers of *karma* so that we can progress rapidly in our devotional service. Unfortunately, most people tend to advance gradually, if at all. When we move too gradually, we may not be able to outrun the material energies that are pursuing us with great intensity.

Everything has a price. In mundane life, the price of a particular goal may be just too high to be worth it. But in spiritual life, the ultimate outcome is eternal love and bliss, for which we must renounce our material attachments and egocentric struggles, which only bring suffering anyway. Is this so difficult?

Think about it. We have been wandering from life to life, from body to body, over and over again, thousands or millions of times. From this perspective if we decide to dedicate this life to ending that process once and for all, we are not sacrificing very much. The attainment of the Kingdom of God is worth whatever price we must pay. Even if we had to live every single day in anxiety and frustration, misunderstood by the entire world, such suffering would be insignificant in comparison to what we would attain eternally.

If the goal were not so wonderful, or if it were not permanent, perhaps the price might be too high. But the endpoint is both wonderful and permanent: no more death, disease, old age, or struggle—just bliss, ecstasy, and constant loving exchanges in the Kingdom of God. We can put all our suffering behind us by dedicating this lifetime to God with no strings attached. Why not do it?

Questions and Answers

Question: The Bible frequently speaks about fearing the Lord. Why is this emphasized?

Answer: There is a difference between heaven and the spiritual realm. The Bible, particularly in its present form, teaches us how to prepare ourselves for heaven, which consists of the higher material planets and the abode of the angels—not the spiritual world, which is the Kingdom of God. The angels do not live in the Kingdom of God. Entrance to this heavenly realm is generally postulated on the idea of fearing the Lord in order to avoid going to hell. That is why so much of the Bible's teaching is about the horrors of hell or the fear of God. If children are insubordinate, one must encourage them to do the right thing to avoid being chastised. That kind of pressure makes them stop and think about what they have done wrong and why they should do the right thing.

Remember that much of the Old Testament narrates the story of the children of Israel who deny the Lord, commit offenses, become hypocritical, indulge themselves, or generally stray from the path of righteousness. Also, one of the basic prayers in the Bible is: "Lord, give us our daily bread." This is not the platform of unconditional, unmotivated love, but rather one of hoping to receive a boon from the Lord in exchange for worship. However, someone who reads the Bible more deeply will gradually come to the point of understanding that "Thy will be done" is the most important prayer of all.

The fire-and-brimstone type of fear has its role, because people who stray from the spiritual path must be motivated to stop their improper behavior before they can understand the need to live in another way. Anticipation of punishment can be a powerful stimulus to changing one's habits.

Question: Each spiritual tradition teaches us to chant in a different way. The Christians, Jews, Muslims, Buddhists, and Hindus all have their own special *mantras*. Which is the correct one?

Answer: Sound itself has an effect on matter and consciousness: it can stimulate, purify, challenge, and elicit attention. When we call someone's name, we are establishing a line of communication and exchange, inviting that person to associate with us. Similarly, as we chant different *mantras*, we are making a spiritual connection.

Mantras are powerful and can act as swords, cutting away negative energy that surrounds us. Different *mantras* have different purposes. Sometimes a spiritual teacher will give the disciple a basic, universal *mantra* that is helpful in almost all situations. At other times, the teacher may provide very specific *mantras* to address a particular circumstance. Practitioners of some traditions chant specific *mantras* to open spiritual ceremonies and others to close them. There are *mantras* for protection, and others to awaken an intimate connection with God.

Members of the Krishna consciousness movement use beads as a support for chanting the *mantra*, just as Muslims, Buddhists, and Catholics do when reciting their particular prayers. The chanting allows the mind to become absorbed in the sound vibration. If we repeat the *mantra* audibly, its vibration enters the ear and has a cleansing effect. If we chant silently, we fix the mind on the *mantra* so it can purify us.

Ma means mind and *tra* means to deliver. The type of *mantra* determines what we are being delivered from. Universal *mantras* that call upon names of the Lord—such as Hare Krishna, Hare Krishna, Krishna Krishna, Hare Hare, Hare Rama, Hare Rama, Rama Rama, Hare Hare—simply mean that we are asking to be released from the material world into the Lord's care and engaged in His service. Such *mantras*, being general appeals to the Divine, are all-inclusive and can help lift us up out of almost any situation. When we rely on these vibrations, we will feel the difference, physically, mentally, and spiritually, because of the *mantra's* power to penetrate various layers of impurity and resistance.

Question: You mentioned that we should always be aware that God is our Father, and that everything belongs to Him. We also hear the same statements in reference to the attainment of earthly wealth: God is our father, and since all the world is His, it is in fact ours, and we can attain it. That creates a paradox for me. Could you please clarify it?

Answer: At different levels of God consciousness, there are different degrees of love. When our love is not deep, we look at the object of our love in terms of what that person can do for us. It is like business. People in such a consciousness can have a kind of devotion to God that sounds like this: "I have prayed; I have meditated; I have chanted; I have made charitable donations. Now, Lord, it's your turn. What are you going to do for me?" This approach is not based on love, but rather on what one can get. As we said earlier, although such an attitude is not at a high level, it is better than no interest in God at all. Gradually, with persistence, the material contamination will be eradicated and the person will gain a more authentic experience of spirituality.

When we approach a fire, at first we get warm, then we get hot, and finally we get burned. The fire absorbs what has entered into it. In a similar way, spiritual life gradually burns away our material desires. The *Bhagavad-gita* explains that even if we still have such desires, we can offer the fruits of our work to the Lord. As we advance further, we follow a progression that moves from working directly on behalf of the Lord to following devotional principles to, eventually, fixing our mind on the Lord and surrendering to Him completely. There is never a time when we have reached the pinnacle of spiritual life; there is always something higher. By increasing our desire to love and serve more, the Lord in our hearts will arrange for these experiences to happen. Transcendental spiritual life is an eternal romance in which every exchange gets explosively sweeter and sweeter.

Closing Reflections

Life is a school of love, and we are made for love. Everyone is starving for love, yet few know how to find it. The worldview of modern culture is an incomplete one, because it fails to see beyond this physical universe and the external phenomena that apparently give our lives meaning. If we consider ourselves to be merely physical creatures who must manipulate our surroundings to survive or to experience any semblance of pleasure, life becomes an endless struggle. Succumbing to our desires, competing for dominance, exploiting one another and our surroundings, trying desperately to grasp as much pleasure as we can—is it any wonder we find life difficult?

Of course we cannot be happy living this way, because we are attempting the impossible. The irony of human existence is that we long for unconditional love, constant bliss, eternal life, and total safety while living in an environment that is indifferent, painful, transitory and dangerous. We cannot gain lasting pleasure, security, and peace from circumstances that are inherently incapable of providing what we want. Why, then, are we so blind to these realities, so persistent in our misdirected quest?

It is not that we must give up our longings. On the contrary, they are legitimate indications that we are meant for something higher and more enduring. Beneath our material coverings, we all know that we are spiritual beings; otherwise, we would not seek conditions so apparently unattainable. We are just looking for them in the wrong direction. Lust is what keeps us bound to this constantly unfulfilled search for lasting pleasure in the material world. Otherwise, we could easily comprehend our situation and make an about-face. Since this is not the case, we must seek help to release ourselves from the illusions that lure us over and over again into the tangled morass of our egocentric desires and deprive us of the eternal love that is our birthright.

Lust is far more than the self-centered desire for sexual pleasure, and sexuality is far broader than the experience of attraction to another person or of physical union. Subtle sex, in which our lust manifests as an all-pervasive desire for adoration, distinction, or profit, lies at the very core of modern society. Without it, would we be so driven to compete against our peers for recognition, manipulate others for financial gain, fight wars to secure control of resources, cover our aging bodies with expensive cosmetics, buy the newest products to keep up with the latest technology, and generally exploit the Earth in support of our wasteful habits?

The ravages of lust are visible everywhere today, and the planet can no longer tolerate the damage. We must find another way. In a very urgent sense, our collective destiny depends upon our ability to transform lust into love. *As Mahatma*

Closing Reflections 255

Gandhi once said, true civilization is not based upon the multiplication of our wants, but in their voluntary restriction. Only then are we free to love and serve one another without selfishness. Simple living and high thinking should be our motto.

In order to restrict our wants willingly, we must believe that giving up our habitual patterns of self-gratification will not deprive us of anything valuable. To get to this point, we must have help. That is why a spiritual support system is so important. Scriptures, spiritual mentors, and daily practices can teach us how to substitute higher, spiritual pleasures for the lower ones that have caused us, and so many others, such intense suffering. As we develop love for God and for all the beings with whom we share this planet, our material desires will gradually fall away by themselves as we experience ever-deepening levels of joy and fulfillment.

Love is an answer to the problems of the world, but it must be love in action, love that offers selfless service to others. The measure of love's sincerity and depth is to be found in our state of consciousness and in our behavior, not in our words or beliefs. As spiritual warriors, we must learn to be available at all times and in all circumstances to say a kind word, defuse a conflict, offer help, and humbly radiate the love that is our growing inner reality.

To be of genuine service, we must be willing to do the necessary inner spiritual work to free ourselves from even the subtlest influences of lust. We cannot give what we do not have, and who we are communicates far more loudly than what we do. If we are to share love with others, we must experience it ourselves. We must become living alternatives to the fearful, competitive mood of society today. As spiritual warriors, we are called upon to uplift the consciousness of all living beings everywhere. Deep compassion is the key. We must stop waiting to be loved, but must give out love. This is something we can do at every moment.

Will you join us, dear reader, in helping to create a culture of love?

Glossary

Akincana: One who possesses nothing in the material world.
Archangel: A chief or principal angel.
Asura: A person opposed to the service of the Lord; a demon.
Bhagavad-gita: The principal scripture of the Vedic tradition presenting the teachings of Lord Krishna to his devotee and friend, Arjuna, and expounding devotion to the Supreme Lord as the highest spiritual perfection. The *Bhagavad-gita* is an episode in the *Mahabharata*, the epic Sanskrit history of the ancient world.
Demigod: A highly evolved being who acts as an agent of the Supreme Lord and is responsible for a particular day-to-day function of this material universe.
Gosvami: A person who has taken vows of renunciation. One who is fully able to control the senses. See also *swami*.
Kali-yuga: The "Age of Quarrel," which began five thousand years ago and lasts a total of 432,000 years. There are four

yugas, which cycle perpetually: Satya-yuga, Treta-yuga, Dvapara-yuga, and Kali-yuga. The good qualities of human beings gradually decline from Satya-yuga to Kali-yuga.

Karma: Material activities, as a consequence of which we incur reactions.

Maya: Illusion; the external energy of the Supreme Lord that deludes living entities into forgetfulness of their spiritual nature and of God.

Nirvana: Freedom from material existence.

Prema: Pure, spontaneous love of and devotion to God.

Rasa: The transcendental "taste" of a particular spiritual relationship with the Supreme Lord.

Rsi: A seer or sage.

Sadhana-bhakti: Spiritual practices.

Samadhi: Trance; complete absorption in God consciousness.

Sac-cid-ananda-vigraha: The Supreme Lord's spiritual body, composed of eternality (*sat*), knowledge (*cit*), and bliss (*ananda*).

Srimad-Bhagavatam: Also known as the *Bhagavata Purana*. An ancient, lengthy Vedic scripture providing narrations and instructions for achieving the highest spiritual goal of love for and devotion to the Supreme Lord. There are eighteen *Puranas*, of which the *Srimad-Bhagavatam* is the most important.

Swami: A person who has taken vows of renunciation. One who is fully able to control the senses. See also *gosvami*.

Yogi: Spiritual renunciate who seeks mystic power. Also refers to spiritual practitioners of various paths such as the path of knowledge (*jnana*), the path of action (*karma*), and the path of devotion (*bhakti*). The *Bhagavad-gita* says that the best *yogi* is one who always thinks of and serves the Supreme Lord with faith and love.

Yuga: Millennium or age. One of the spiritual seasons that occur on a cyclical basis in this universe.

Yuga-dharma: The appropriate religion or spiritual practice for a particular millennium.

Endnotes

[1] For a more extensive discussion of the spiritual aspects of leadership today, see one of the author's earlier books, *Leadership for an Age of Higher Consciousness*.

[2] Quoted by Dinadayadri Dasi in "Memories of Srila Prabhupada—Part 37"

[3] James Patterson and Peter Kim, *The Day America Told the Truth* (New York: Prentice Hall Press, 1991): 94.

[4] Ibid, 96.

[5] Brendan I. Koerner, "Porn Dot Com: A Lust for Profits," *U.S. News and World Report* (March 27, 2000): 36 -38, 40, 42, 44.

Index

Abuses of power, 43
Acarya, 17
Adventure, 8, 22, 122, 171
Association, 23, 67, 105, 128, 205
Atheism, 21, 22
Bhagavad-gita, 30, 73, 74, 78, 85, 90, 112, 118, 240, 251
Bhukti, 24
Bliss, 5, 51, 60, 116, 120, 148, 234, 248, 253
Boundaries
  importance of, 46
Challenges, 20, 22, 25, 27, 34, 71, 85, 87, 88, 110, 157, 171, 194, 209
Chant, 21, 87, 110, 119, 131, 165, 220, 250
Cheaters, 18, 45, 93
Children, 10, 20, 22, 30, 33, 45, 46, 63, 68, 69, 87, 96, 125, 129, 133, 135, 140, 141, 158, 159, 160, 164, 167, 168, 175, 176, 179, 180, 191, 196, 199, 209, 212, 213, 218, 228, 229, 230, 231, 239, 249
Christians, 4, 62, 239, 242
Compassion, 11, 32, 34, 84, 135, 136, 166, 173, 177, 197, 198, 199, 201, 202, 203, 204, 205, 206, 207, 208, 209, 210, 214, 215, 217, 218, 219, 220, 221, 223, 225, 235, 246, 255
Competition, 10, 94, 146, 166, 237
Conflict, 27, 155, 176, 212
Confronting, 9
Death, 25, 43, 50, 60, 75, 92, 99, 114, 188, 208, 210, 212, 224, 228, 243, 248
Dependence on the Lord, 25
Depression, 15, 151
Destruction, 9, 42, 177, 188
Emotions, 14, 20, 188, 191

261

Emptiness, 16, 170, 188
Enemies, 11, 55, 78, 82, 83, 84, 85, 105
Energy, 24, 28, 29, 31, 32, 35, 39, 40, 41, 43, 44, 45, 47, 48, 51, 59, 60, 64, 66, 74, 77, 82, 93, 100, 110, 122, 125, 126, 127, 128, 133, 134, 135, 136, 137, 140, 141, 142, 143, 148, 150, 153, 154, 158, 161, 164, 174, 182, 189, 194, 195, 202, 205, 215, 216, 217, 219, 220, 221, 222, 223, 224, 231, 232, 233, 238, 239, 241, 243, 248, 250
Enjoyment, 24, 55, 65, 100, 236, 244
Enthusiasm, 16, 111, 122, 178
Excitement, 22, 49
Expectations, 20, 188, 192
Exploitation, 10, 28, 30, 32, 33, 34, 43, 45, 46, 53, 125, 137, 154
Failure, 9, 23, 40, 128, 146
Families, 4, 31, 38, 40, 43, 44, 45, 80, 135, 174, 175
Famine, 9
Fear, 22, 45, 146, 153, 165, 178, 190, 198, 205, 207, 215, 230, 231, 249
Finances, 21
Floods, 9, 173
Forgetfulness, 15, 22, 25, 211
Friendship, 16, 22, 33, 73, 87, 101, 105, 106, 120, 178, 186, 208, 228, 239
Fulfillment, 10, 20, 21, 27, 51, 137, 138, 150, 162, 164, 170, 195, 215, 239, 255
Happiness, 10, 13, 20, 21, 22, 52, 55, 56, 57, 76, 89, 92, 93, 102, 106, 118, 166, 167, 168, 174, 188, 204, 214, 237, 244
Homosexuality
   spiritual aspects of, 34

Hypocrisy, 42, 96
Illness, 4, 113, 173, 208, 222
Illusion, 11, 17, 58, 77, 82, 92, 95, 101, 149, 156, 194, 195, 239, 240, 254
Illustrated Bhagavatam Stories, 1
Inadequacy
   of leaders, 187, 188
India, 8, 61, 135, 242
Insecurity, 22
Issues, 7, 41, 44, 102, 155, 158
Kama-sutra, 32
Karma, 33, 66, 102, 132, 169, 194, 216, 222, 248
Knowledge, 4, 5, 8, 10, 11, 13, 51, 60, 62, 65, 66, 71, 84, 96, 119, 134, 137, 143, 180, 227, 234, 235, 236, 238, 244, 247
Leaders, 29
   dangers for, 44, 46
   developing, 47
   examples of, 11, 44
   need for, 11, 28
   proper role of, 44, 45, 46, 47
   shortcomings of, 29, 37, 39, 44, 45, 50
   strong, 42
   we are all, 11
Leadership
   spiritual, 45
Love
   and happiness, 20
   becoming lovers, 11, 25, 171, 228, 242
   is not always pleasant, 55
   is stronger than doubt, 57
   school of, 15
   source of, 58
   ultimate lover, 146, 171, 242, 244
Meditation, 21, 116, 138, 163, 220, 242
Misdirected sexual energy, 31
Money, 10, 18, 19, 50, 57, 71, 87, 88, 101, 113, 158, 173, 195, 199, 213

Mukti, 24
Opportunity, 10, 14, 15, 16, 20, 21, 22, 26, 41, 49, 54, 56, 61, 83, 85, 87, 90, 92, 108, 129, 139, 151, 157, 158, 165, 215, 216
Parenthood, 20
Parents, 16, 37, 45, 46, 68, 130, 131, 132, 133, 160, 179, 197, 213, 228, 230, 231
Pleasure, 3, 39, 53, 55, 67, 79, 80, 92, 100, 104, 117, 118, 123, 128, 137, 146, 151, 171, 233, 236, 237, 244, 253, 254
Prabhupada, 117, 258
Prestige, 27, 39, 52, 93
Principles
 divine, 30, 240
Productivity, 19, 43
Progress, 9, 23, 47, 58, 66, 87, 100, 102, 104, 105, 109, 132, 153, 181, 183, 194, 247, 248
Promiscuity, 29, 31, 43, 103, 104, 143
Purity, 21
Rape, 30, 31, 174
Relationships
 impediments to, 45
 improving, 40, 48, 55
 in the media, 30
 purpose, 21
 seeking, 51, 54
 ultimate, 24
Religion, 4, 14, 15, 42, 62, 70, 214, 232
Sac-cid-ananda-vigraha, 60
Sadhana-bhakti, 21
Selfishness, 17, 125, 204, 215, 246, 255
Sexual energy, 40, 128
Sexuality
 and abuse, 10, 53
 dangers of, 28, 29, 31
 developing sexual energies, 29, 41, 48

esoteric, 36, 37
 healthy, 49
 imbalance, 35
 manipulation through, 30, 45
 power of, 31, 49
 subtle, 30, 49, 50, 53
 unhealthy, 39
Society
 encourages sense gratification, 30
Solace, 8
Spirituality, 19, 20, 62, 67, 76, 77, 142, 159, 181, 214, 215, 229, 233, 234, 235, 241, 246, 251
Srimad-Bhagavatam, 61, 67, 227
Stagnancy, 26
Subtle sex, 39
Success, 4, 28, 49, 57, 120, 161, 192
Terrorism, 9
Tritiya-prakriti, 32
Truth, 4, 5, 46, 61, 73, 76, 123, 127, 148, 157, 179, 180, 201, 216, 223, 227, 229, 234
Utopia, 5
Voltaire, 28
Vulnerabilities, 32, 43, 56, 58, 188
Warrior, 3, 4, 7, 8, 10, 11, 56, 66, 82, 97, 109, 166, 177, 178, 183, 185, 187, 188, 189, 190, 191, 192, 193, 203, 207, 214, 217, 255
Wealth, 4, 52, 93, 113, 188, 251
Wisdom, 16, 45, 47, 116, 206
Yogis, 61, 66, 138

 About the Author

Bhakti-Tirtha Swami Krishnapada was born John E. Favors in a pious, God-fearing family. As a child evangelist he appeared regularly on television. As a young man he was a leader in Dr. Martin Luther King, Jr.'s civil rights movement. At Princeton University he became president of the student council and also served as chairman of the Third World Coalition. Although his main degree is in psychology, he has received accolades in many other fields, including politics, African studies, and international law.

Bhakti-Tirtha Swami's books are used as reference texts in universities and leadership organizations throughout the world. Many of his books have been printed in English, German, French, Spanish, Portuguese, Macedonian, Croatian, Russian, Hebrew, Slovenian, Balinese and Italian.

His Holiness has served as Assistant Coordinator for penal reform programs in the State of New Jersey, Office of the Public

Defender, and as a director of several drug abuse clinics in the United States. In addition, he has been a special consultant for Educational Testing Services in the U.S.A. and has managed campaigns for politicians. Bhakti-Tirtha Swami gained international recognition as a representative of the Bhaktivedanta Book Trust, particularly for his outstanding work with scholars in the former communist countries of Eastern Europe.

Bhakti-Tirtha Swami directly oversees projects in the United States (particularly Washington D.C., Potomac, Maryland, Detroit, Pennsylvania, West Virginia), West Africa, South Africa, Switzerland, France, Croatia and Bosnia. He also serves as the director of the American Federation of Vaisnava Colleges and Schools.

In the United States, Bhakti-Tirtha Swami is the founder and director of the Institute for Applied Spiritual Technology, director of the International Committee for Urban Spiritual Development and one of the international coordinators of the Seventh Pan African Congress. Reflecting his wide range of interests, he is also a member of the Institute for Noetic Sciences, the Center for Defense Information, the United Nations Association for America, the National Peace Institute Foundation, the World Future Society and the Global Forum of Spiritual and Parliamentary Leaders.

A specialist in international relations and conflict resolution, Bhakti-Tirtha Swami constantly travels around the world and has become a spiritual consultant to many high-ranking members of the United Nations, to various celebrities and to several chiefs, kings and high court justices. In 1990 His Holiness was coronated as a high chief in Warri, Nigeria in recognition of his outstanding work in Africa and the world. In recent years, he has met several times with then-President Nelson Mandela of South Africa to share visions and strategies for world peace.

In addition to encouraging self-sufficiency through the development of schools, clinics, farm projects and cottage industries, Bhakti-Tirtha Swami conducts seminars and workshops on principle centered leadership, spiritual development, interpersonal relationships, stress and time management and other pertinent topics. He is also widely acknowledged as a viable participant in the resolution of global conflict.

Printed in Great Britain
by Amazon